GW01035011

**Community Care
Practice Handbooks**

General Editor: Martin Davies

Social Inquiry Reports

Community Care
Practice Handbooks

General Editor: Martin Davies

Social Inquiry Reports

A Framework for Practice
Development

Anthony Bottoms and
Andrew Stelman

Published by
Wildwood House Limited
Gower House
Croft Road
Aldershot
Hants GU11 3HR
England

Distributed by
Gower Publishing Company
Old Post Road
Brookfield
Vermont 05036
USA

British Library Cataloguing in Publication Data
Bottoms, A.E. (Anthony Edward), 1939 -
    Social inquiry reports: a framework for practice development. -
    (Community care practice handbooks; 29).
    1. Great Britain. Criminal courts. Social inquiry reports. Preparation
    I. Title II. Stelman, Andrew III. Series
    344.105'77

Library of Congress Cataloguing-in-Publication Data
Bottoms, A.E.
    Social inquiry reports : a framework for practice development /
    Anthony Bottoms and Andrew Stelman.
    p. cm. -- (Community care practice handbooks ; 29)
    Bibliography: p. Includes index.
    1. Pre-sentence investigation reports -- Great Britain.
    I. Stelman, Andrew, 1948-   . II. Title. III. Series.
    HV9345.A5B65   1988
    364.6'5–dc 19   88-17472

ISBN 0 7045 0579 7

Printed and bound in Great Britain at
The Camelot Press Ltd, Southampton

Contents

Preface

This book evolved out of an unusual experience. In the autumn of 1980, one of the authors (AEB) was invited to address the annual conference of Chief Probation Officers, whose theme that year was 'The Court, the Probation Officer, and Non-Custodial Measures'. In the course of this address, the topic of social inquiry reports (SIRs) was touched upon in a way that interested the probation service's Northern Regional Staff Development Officer. An invitation from him followed to develop a course on this subject for northern region probation officers. For the next three years (1981-84) two-part courses on social inquiry practice were run, under the leadership of Peter Warburton, Chief Probation Officer for County Durham, with the principal theoretical input coming from Tony Bottoms. In each course, participants were encouraged to test out ideas from the first part of the course in their own workplace before returning for the second part.

What emerged at the end of three years bore a resemblance to, but was certainly not the same as, the initial theoretical sketch which had been presented to the first course. All kinds of issues were raised by the participants, from fundamental theoretical matters about the nature of the SIR, to very practical issues about difficulties in particular local courts. Thus the initial theory was modified in the light of the collective experience of course members. At the end of the third course, in 1984, one group of course participants strongly urged that a book should be written for practitioners, setting out clearly some of the main ideas which had been developed on the course.

A little belatedly, this book is an attempt to meet this request. In writing it, we have of course had to take into account developments since 1984, and we have also further refined some of the ideas originally presented in the course; but the basic framework remains unchanged.

The book is, quite deliberately, co-authored by an academic (AEB) and a practitioner (AES). It is primarily intended as a book for practitioners (and social work students), but its contents reflect our firm belief that good practice needs to be informed by sound theory – that, in the famous saying, 'there is nothing so practical as a good theory'. Yet although intended as a book for practitioners, readers will not find here – as they will, for example, in the recent DHSS booklet – practical advice on such matters as how to lay out the front page of a report, how to list the investigations upon which the report is based, or the problems of hearsay evidence (see DHSS 1987, paras 20, 22, 54). Advice on such matters can readily be sought elsewhere. Our intention has been to provide a *framework of analysis* which will guide good practice: we believe there is, at the present time, a clear need for such a framework.

Because the book is not primarily intended for an academic audience, we have made no attempt to cover all aspects of the research literature on SIRs. Readers who are interested in this topic should consult, in the first instance, the essay by Tony Bottoms and Bill McWilliams in the festschrift for Barbara Wootton, which aims to review the main British research on SIRs up to 1985 (Bottoms and McWilliams 1986).

It is appropriate to add a word on the important question of gender. Throughout the text, we have for convenience designated the report writer as female and the defendant as male, but our suggestions are intended to apply as much to SIRs written on female offenders as on males. We are aware of the recent research which suggests that the gender of the defendant does not appear to influence the sentence recommended in SIRs, but that probation officers may nevertheless make more home visits on female than on male subjects of SIRs, and may also present the details of home circumstances in a different way for males and females (Eaton 1985; 1986, Chapter 5). We can see no justification for these differences, which need to be guarded against. The basic principles of SIR preparation and writing should be the same whether the defendant is female or male.

Anthony Bottoms
Andrew Stelman

Acknowledgements

There are many people and organizations we would like to thank: Northern Regional Staff Development Office for its imagination in setting the whole thing in motion, and its willingness to sustain it.

The course staff and course members of three RSDO residential courses, especially Peter Warburton, Eddie Burfitt, Evelyn Dalton, Barry Keane and Michael Mulvany.

The University of Cambridge Institute of Criminology and the Cropwood Trust, for the award of a Cropwood Fellowship to AES which enabled the work to be completed.

The Nottinghamshire Probation Service for allowing AES to undertake the Cropwood Fellowship, and particularly the whole of the North Nottinghamshire probation team for its help and good-humoured forbearance towards what may often have seemed like an obsession.

Fitzwilliam College, Cambridge for its hospitality.

Bill McWilliams and Eric Sainsbury, whose work and enthusiastic encouragement have been a constant source of inspiration.

Kay Foad for her constructively critical comments on the first draft.

Pamela Paige, who with unfailing tolerance turned many scribbled drafts into a presentable final manuscript.

Maggie, Amy, Hannah and Ruth who have put up with AES's long absences, and have made his homecomings such joyful occasions.

1 Policy developments and practice issues

PO: Well, having thought about what we talked of last week, it's on the cards that the magistrates might send you to a detention centre.

Colin: [loudly, and suddenly sitting upright] Why? Is that what you think? Is that in your report?... So you'll say 'get him sent down'!

PO: [a bit flustered] No! I'm just looking at the facts to help the magistrates. You haven't let me finish. I don't say what sentence the magistrates will pass ... I don't feel that detention centre would be good for you.

Colin: Why are you putting it in *there* then? [pointing at the papers the PO is holding].

PO: I'm *not*! [vehemently] ... I'm wanting to suggest an alternative to detention centre ... to suggest something else. Because I don't think a detention centre would be good for you, I'm going to recommend a probation order as an alternative. I just want to be realistic with you.

[The PO went on to explain something of the reporting requirements of the probation order and then said:]

PO: You've got to consent.

Colin: If it comes to a choice, I'm not going to say DC, am I? [laughs].

PO: Do you know what probation involves?

Colin: No, but it's better than DC.

PO: Probation can help too, Colin ... you've got to report ... we can also offer help as well ... Do you think you would like to be on probation?

Colin: Well, I can't say until I've tried.

PO: Detention centre would really be unsuitable.

Colin: I understand you've got a job to do.[1]

The dialogue reported above will probably sound familiar to many probation officers, and others who write social inquiry reports (SIRs). It will, we think, be instantly recognizable as the kind of discussion which goes on – day in, day out – as the routine business of preparing SIRs is carried out all over the country.

Our aim in this book is to provide an analytic framework which will be of help to report writers in their daily work. The framework which we offer – and the different professional backgrounds which we bring to the book – reflect our view that good practice emerges from an amalgam of sound theory; a defensible value-commitment; an understanding of the current context (official guidelines and the like); and practical knowledge and skills.

The book is structured in the following way. In the rest of this chapter the changing context of report writing in the 1980s is examined; three reports are presented for critical scrutiny; and some key dilemmas familiar to all practitioners are identified. Chapter 2 considers three theoretical approaches to report writing, while Chapter 3 firmly identifies report writing as a social work activity. These first three chapters then act as a springboard for a discussion of SIR content and practice, which is contained in Chapters 4, 5, and 6. Chapter 7 concludes the book with a discussion about the agency and court contexts within which report writing takes place, and some ways in which organizations can sanction, reinforce, and support appropriate kinds of practice.

Developments in SIR policy in the 1980s
The kind of SIR practice which we recommend has much in common with, though also some differences from, other developments in SIR writing which have taken place in the 1980s. It is important, therefore, that our discussion should be set in an appropriate context by considering these developments at the outset. Later in this chapter, some actual SIRs, written in 1982, are considered.

There is evidence that, in England and Wales, we are living through a time of change in the nature of SIRs being prepared for the criminal courts. From a postal survey of local probation services carried out in 1985, Howard Parker, Graham Jarvis and Maggie Sumner (1987, p.28) reported two major recent trends in policy. First, there was a significant shift in the kind of cases in which SIRs were prepared:

> Generally the trend is away from the preparation of reports on first-time offenders ... and away from pre-trial reports ... towards an emphasis on reports on those at risk of high-tariff sentences.

Secondly, the authors noted some evidence of a change in the content of reports towards:

> firmer recommendations... and, more strikingly, a particular emphasis on alternatives to custody in almost half [the areas of] the Service, and with nearly a fifth [of areas] adopting a policy of not recommending custody at all.

This survey by Parker and his colleagues relied upon responses from senior managers in different probation areas, and it is almost certain that ground-level practice is not always consistent with expressed management policy. It is also highly probable that practice varies a

good deal within areas. Nevertheless, our knowledge of the probation service, and of local authority social service departments,
suggests to us that the broad trends in SIR development in the 1980s
are indeed as Parker and his colleagues described them. These trends,
we believe, have been particularly influenced by five identifiable
events taking place in the 1980s, namely: the Criminal Justice Act
1982; the Home Office 'Statement of National Objectives and Priorities for the Probation Service in England and Wales', 1984; Home
Office Circulars on SIRs in 1983 and 1986; the DHSS booklet on
Reports to Courts: Practice Guidance for Social Workers published
in 1987; and some special local initiatives. Each of these needs to be
explained briefly.

The Criminal Justice Act 1982 is of importance to the SIR in two
ways. First, the Act, by s.1(4), provides that the court may not pass
a custodial sentence on an offender under the age of 21 'unless it is
of the opinion that no other method of dealing with him is appropriate', and for the purpose of judging 'appropriateness', three tests are
laid down, one of which is that 'it appears to the court that he is unable
or unwilling to respond to non-custodial penalties'.[2] This is then
backed up by s.2 of the Act, which provides that, in the usual case, the
court must obtain an SIR for the purpose of determining whether the
criteria of s.1(4) are met.[3]

Although research evidence strongly suggests that magistrates'
and juvenile courts, at least, do not always pay detailed attention to
the wording of s.1(4) (Burney 1985a, 1985b; Reynolds 1985;
Whitehead and Macmillan 1985), and national custodial rates for the
under 21 age group have altered little since the implementation of the
Act in 1983, nevertheless there seems little doubt that the Act did
provide a stimulus for many probation services and local authority
services departments to consider more actively how they could
provide better quality SIRs for those at real risk of a custodial
sentence. Thus the Act encouraged local services to 'review one area
of practice which [had] remained in a relative backwater for the past
twenty-five years' (Tutt and Giller 1985).[4]

The second relevant feature of the 1982 Act is to be found in the
area of supervisory orders. Schedule 11 of the Act remodelled some
of the statutory provisions relating to requirements in probation
orders, and enacted, mostly for offenders in a relatively high position
on the tariff, new provisions known as 4A and 4B requirements.[5] For
both these kinds of requirements there are statutory provisions
making it mandatory for the court to consult a probation officer
before inserting the requirement into the probation order[6] and a

Home Office Circular has advised that these statutory provisions should normally be met by the court requesting an SIR, and then hearing any additional oral evidence which may be necessary in the circumstances of the case (HOC 4/1983, para. 10).

For juvenile offenders, the Act also contains (for somewhat different reasons) a remodelling of the provisions relating to requirements in supervision orders, again with some emphasis on high-tariff offenders; and before making any of these requirements (the so-called 3C requirements[7]) a social worker or probation officer must be consulted as to the offender's circumstances, and the feasibility of securing compliance with the requirements. Additionally, the court may not include any 3C requirement in a supervision order unless it considers that the requirement is 'necessary for securing the good conduct of the supervised person or for preventing a repetition' of offending. In determining this issue, the court may need to take account of the contents of an SIR. It will be observed that some of these matters, like the provisions of s.1(4) about custodial sentences for those under the age of 21 (see above), are quite specific: Henri Giller (in Tutt and Giller 1984), noting these matters, has therefore commented that the Act 'begins to point report writers towards consideration of particular concrete issues', such as whether the offender is able to respond to a particular non-custodial sentence (under s.1(4)), or whether a juvenile offender's circumstances are such as to make his compliance feasible in a supervised activities requirement under s.12(3C) (a) of the Children and Young Persons Act 1969.[8]

Giller is undoubtedly right in theory, but we doubt whether many probation officers and social workers have taken sufficient notice of the statutory wording to make this specificity much of a practical reality in most areas. Nevertheless, the Criminal Justice Act's provision for new high-tariff requirements in both probation and supervision orders has undoubtedly provided a spur to local services to concentrate attention, in local practice, on the provision of practical 'alternatives to custody' and on what kind of SIR writing should accompany such provision.

The second major influence upon change in SIR practice in the 1980s has been the Home Office's 1984 'Statement of National Objectives and Priorities for the Probation Service in England and Wales' (reprinted in Walker 1985, Appendix H). In seeking effectiveness, relevance, and value for money in the probation service, and some redistribution of resources (section VII), the Statement offered guidance to local areas on a number of practice issues. So far as working with the courts was concerned, the Statement recommended the following:

(i) concentrating the provision of social inquiry reports on cases where a report is statutorily required, where a probation order is likely to be considered, and where the court may be prepared to divert an offender from what would otherwise be a custodial sentence;
(ii) maintaining the confidence of the courts in the ability of non-custodial measures to cope with a wide range of offenders.

Given the Home Office's concurrent Financial Management Initiative (FMI), with its accompanying financial stringency, the clear implied message of the Statement is that local probation services should concentrate their activities on relatively high-tariff offenders, and then (given the resource constraints) abandon practices such as the routine provision of reports on first offenders appearing before the juvenile court (still prevalent until recently in many areas).

The Statement considered the type of offender about whom reports should be prepared (see above), but it gave no guidance on the content of SIRs. The Home Office has, however, provided such guidance on two separate occasions in the 1980s, in the form of Home Office Circulars. First, in February 1983 two Circulars were issued simultaneously, one on the general contents of SIRs, and one specifically on recommendations as to sentence (Home Office Circulars 17/1983 and 18/1983). The main thrust of these Circulars was towards greater specificity. Thus, the first Circular sees advantage in the report writer 'concentrating primarily on a limited number of subjects which are essential for the court's consideration', and warns that, 'only information which is clearly relevant should be included' (HOC 17/1983, para. 3). The report, it is said, should give 'a clear indication of the sources on which the author has drawn' (HOC 17/1983, paras 5, 6).

As for the recommendation, the second Circular (HOC 18/1983) suggests that this is:

likely to be more helpful, and carry more weight, if it is *supported with reasons* related to the consequences which the probation officer's experience indicates are likely to follow if the course recommended is – or is not – taken. For example, if a probation order is recommended, it is useful for the court to be told, in *terms that are as specific as possible*, how probation may be expected to affect the offender's conduct or environment. (para. 4) [emphasis added]

In December 1986, the Home Office thought it right to provide further guidance on SIRs. Home Office Circular 92/1986 builds on the 1983 Circulars, and incorporates some features of them. Four features of the new Circular are worth commenting on specifically. First, the Circular reinforces the implied message of the Statement of National Objectives and Priorities by stating explicitly that reports 'should not be prepared as a matter of course in respect of relatively minor offences, unless the defendant is, or recently has been subject to supervision' (para. 17)[9]. Secondly, for the first time in official guidance on SIRs, cultural factors are stressed; we are told that information in the report might include:

> the nature of the community in which he or she lives, with particular attention to any cultural factors which may be relevant (para.10 (iii))

and

> in considering cases involving members of ethnic minorities it is especially important to bring out any significant aspects of the defendant's social or cultural background which may not otherwise be understood by the court. (para.11)

Thirdly, the 1986 Circular places a great deal of stress on the current offence and the defendant's offending history. Hence we are told that:

> the feature which distinguishes [the Social Inquiry Report] from other reports is that it should set the offending behaviour into the individual's social context, examine the offender's view of such behaviour, and assess the likely effect of the range of measures available to the court on the offender and any dependants. (para. 5)

or again

> a Social Inquiry Report comments upon the social factors *only to the extent that they are relevant to the particular offender and offences before the court*. (para. 24) [emphasis added]

The report should also, it is said, 'provide adequate interpretation of or comment upon the criminal history of the defendant' (para. 10).

Fourthly, and following on from the above, the 1986 Circular takes the view that, given the centrality of the offending focus in its approach to SIR writing, there are obvious difficulties in preparing such reports where the defendant is intending to plead not guilty. The Circular therefore recommends avoiding this practice in magistrates' courts and, in the Crown Court, discussing the issue with the local presiding judge with a view to making local arrangements (although 'the principles indicated ... still apply' (paras 18-19).[10]

The Home Office has, of course, no constitutional authority to offer advice on report writing to local authority social workers in their work with juvenile offenders. The DHSS has therefore followed up the 1986 Home Office Circular with a comprehensive practice guidance booklet entitled *Reports to Courts: Practice Guidance for Social Workers* (DHSS 1987). Some sections of this booklet deal with matters outside our present concerns, such as welfare reports in care and in matrimonial proceedings. The sections on SIRs tend to follow very much (and in some instances to state more sharply) the earlier Home Office guidance. Thus, for example, routine pre-trial reports are not recommended (paras 2, 140-42); it is stated clearly that 'the primary focus of a report should be on offending' and that 'detailed comment on the current offence is ... central to the report' (paras 102-103); and it is suggested that reports in not guilty cases should be avoided since reports cannot be offence focused if the child denies the offence (para.140). The booklet also draws out the implications of this general approach in some other important areas. For example, with regard to family history and relationships, it is said that in day-to-day practice these sections of reports 'perhaps show the greatest tendency to stray from a focused approach' (para. 60). The DHSS therefore argues that:

> it is not the task of the writer to refer to marital problems whenever they exist – some discord exists in most marriages – but only to make reference where there is a clear link between the discord and the problem which has brought the child to the court. (para. 60)

To conclude this brief review of the main features of change in SIRs in the 1980s, we must mention some local developments which have had an impact and influence beyond their own area. In the probation service a particular influence has come from the Demonstration Unit of the Inner London Probation Service who worked with young adult offenders with several convictions for burglary or taking and driving away. Their SIR interviews were much more offence-focused than had been the previous practice of the officers concerned, and their final reports contained 'much more comment about the offence and the client's past and present offending behaviour', with concomitantly a 'lesser amount of personal background information' (Harraway *et al.* 1985). Commenting on the experience of the Demonstration Unit and other local projects, John Harding (1987, pp.5-6), Chief Probation Officer for Hampshire, argues that:

> to gain a 'market share' of custody it is especially important that the

probation officer writing a Social Inquiry Report concentrates on an analysis of the subject's offending behaviour, details the likely impact of certain options before the sentencing court, and finally recommends a disposal that is designed in terms of regime, programme content and accountability procedures to reduce crime.[11]

Local initiatives have also proved important as regards the target group for reports.The Greater Manchester Probation Service, for example, decided not to write SIRs on first-time offenders in the juvenile court, and subsequently second-timers unless specifically requested by the court. The result was a greater use of nominal penalties (fines and discharges) by the court (Tutt and Giller 1985). The Manchester experience was then used as an example by others who believed that the practice of routinely providing reports on first-timers could have the unintended effect of pushing offenders up the juvenile justice tariff more quickly.[12]

Also in the sphere of juvenile justice, some local areas have developed quite complex overall strategies for SIR work, including changes in the content of individual SIRs; changes in the way in which SIRs are organizationally managed within the agency (social services or probation); and changes in the total 'systems context' (that is, links to other significant parts of the criminal justice system) in which they are received (Tutt and Giller 1984; Morris and Giller 1987, pp. 218-28). These changes have included such matters as the production of local notes of guidance on SIR preparation; internal organizational arrangements in social services departments whereby senior officers can review the content of, and recommendations in, SIRs before they are submitted to the court (often known as 'gatekeeping' strategies); discussion with the local education authority about the consistency of information appearing respectively in the school report and the SIR; and discussion with magistrates so that they are aware of the changes in report writing that are taking place. As regards the content of reports (the main focus of this book), the usual policy in the local areas which have pioneered these developments is, once again, to place great stress upon the offence, as in the following example:

> A recommended format of the style and content of Social Inquiry Reports is outlined below. It will be noted that it differs significantly from the style adopted previously in Social Inquiry Reports. These tended to concentrate upon the personality, early history, and welfare of the young offender and his family. Social Inquiry Reports are now seen as documents to assist the court in deciding the appropriate sanction for the offender. Thus, the report must concentrate upon the offence, the

circumstances surrounding it, and the offender's involvement in it, his attitude towards it, and his likely compliance with the recommendation which is put forward.

The theoretical basis of policies such as these will be discussed in the next chapter.

Three social inquiry reports

Since this book is about SIR practice, we thought it important to include some examples of practice in the introductory chapter.

Three SIRs are reproduced below. They were written in 1982, and therefore pre-date the policy developments outlined in the previous section. They were first selected at random, as part of a training exercise on the 1982 RSDO course (see Preface); they were not chosen as examples of especially good or especially bad practice.[13]

Three reports cannot represent all reports; and in any case, from the document itself one cannot always appreciate all the processes that lie behind it, nor of course how it was presented and received in court. Nevertheless, a close look at some actual reports of a relatively recent date does have a value in reminding us what, in broad terms, SIR writing looked like immediately before the policy changes outlined in the previous paragraphs and, given the gap between policy and practice, what it perhaps still looks like in some places.

Case A (Magistrates' Court)

Name: Andrew Bishop (aged 49)
Offence: Assist in handling stolen goods

1   Andrew Bishop is a married man and the father of four children. His eldest son (25) is married and lives in Eastleigh. The other three children, 20, 16 and 13, are all still living at home with the elder two working at a local bakery. Mr and Mrs Bishop have been married since 1955 and the marriage appears a happy one. Mrs Bishop also works part-time at the local bakery.

2   Mr Bishop and his family live in a three-bedroomed council property which they have occupied since September 1981, and in which standards of decor and furnishings are high.

3   Mr Bishop has lived in the Scisset area all his life and was the youngest in a family of three members. He was educated locally and left school in 1948 at the age of 15 years. As a youngster he was interested in sport and recalled playing for Scisset boys club at football. This interest in sport has been maintained through his eldest son who is a part-time professional boxer.

4   On leaving school, Mr Bishop secured a job as a painter and decorator with the local council. At 18, he was called up for National Service; his army service was spent in the Royal Artillery and during the two-year period of

duty, Mr Bishop was posted to Hong Kong for most of the time.

5 In 1953, Mr Bishop returned to civilian life and obtained employment, initially with a firm of civil engineering sub-contractors. He later obtained work with the Electricity Board, and finally with the National Coal Board at Skelmanthorpe colliery. He worked at each of these for several years, but was forced to leave the National Coal Board in 1974 after suffering a back injury following a fall. This condition of sciatica has, however, improved to the extent now that Mr Bishop no longer requires treatment, but he does still experience some pain.

6 Mr Bishop began working for the Prova Security Services Ltd in August 1977, but in December 1977 Mr Bishop made his first court appearance at the Scisset Crown Court. This was for the offences of theft and burglary for which Mr Bishop received six months' imprisonment.

7 In conversation, Mr Bishop impresses as a mature and sensible family man whose previous taste of imprisonment has had a profound effect upon him. Mr Bishop is painfully aware of the upset and worry he has caused his family for what, in essence, constitutes such a minor lapse on his part. Mr Bishop fully realises how thoughtlessly he behaved and is adamant that in future he would report to the police any approach. In view then of Mr Bishop's good character and circumstances surrounding the offence, I would suggest that the court impose a financial penalty today as the most appropriate punishment.

Case B (Magistrates' Court)
Name: Barry Davenport (aged 17)
Offences: 1 Drive whilst disqualified
         2 No insurance
         3 No test certificate
(This report is based on information supplied by the defendant and his mother. I have also had access to the file kept by the Social Services Department, a Care Order still being in force.)
Family structure:
Father: Thomas Davenport, cohabiting in Birmingham
Mother: June Davenport, 256 Birch Avenue, Blackton
Half-brother: Andrew Smith, 256 Birch Avenue, Blackton (recently discharged from prison)
Half-brother: Arthur Smith, currently in HM Prison Dartmoor
Subject: Barry Davenport, unemployed
Accommodation:
A four bedroomed modern council flat on the Mount estate in Blackton. It is well furnished and maintained.
Family background:
The family has been known to social work agencies since 1965. Mrs Davenport (then Mrs Smith) had separated from her husband two years earlier; there are two children of the marriage, Andrew and Arthur. A long-

standing but frequently interrupted cohabitation then commenced with Mr Davenport, father of Barry. It was a turbulent relationship, with frequent allegations of physical violence towards Mrs Davenport; also there were severe financial problems. In March 1966 the family was evicted from lodgings and the three children were received into care and remained in residential care for the next six years. For the final two years of this period there was no contact with the children by the mother, and none by either father for the whole period.

In 1973 Arthur, Andrew and Barry were placed with foster parents where they quickly settled and remained there up to January 1978. Again there was no contact made by the parents. The period of foster care ended abruptly when allegations were made by Barry's half-brother of sexual assault by the male foster parent. He was charged and found guilty of such assault and sent to prison. The three boys were then separated, with Barry being placed in a residential home in Dunford Valley where he remained until May 1979. Andrew, and Arthur to a much lesser degree, became involved in criminal activities and both have served custodial sentences.

In June 1978 Barry's parents married and Mrs Davenport had re-established contact with Barry. He hoped desperately that his parents would remain together and that he would eventually be able to return home. Unfortunately Mr Davenport left home yet again, and commenced his current cohabitation in Birmingham. Barry was discharged from the residential home to his mother in May 1979, later he lived with a family friend.

During his thirteen year period in both residential and foster care Barry presented few problems. His school attendance and performance was always satisfactory; he was co-operative and compliant. His behaviour following his return home gave little cause for concern until March 1980 when he was involved in an episode of shoplifting in Greenton and received an official caution. This was followed by a further shoplifting offence in Woodborough in May 1980 and he was fined. He left school in May 1980 and in October 1980 he worked for a transport firm in the stores under the Work Experience Programme. This ended in February 1981. He has tried to find other work since but without success. He receives £16.85 a week in DHSS benefit, £15 of which he gives to his mother for his keep. His leisure interests are almost entirely concentrated on motor cars, though he has some interest in records and spending time with friends in Scisset.

Since returning to live with his mother almost twelve months ago Barry's behaviour and attitude has improved considerably and he appears to be maturing. His fascination for cars means that he is always at risk of traffic offences but it is hoped that he can exercise more self-restraint in future.

Today's court appearance results from his driving an old car which he owned at the time. It had been vandalized and moved by some youths and Barry's explanation is that he was merely returning it to its former parking ground.

Barry's life has been far from straightforward and his background evokes sympathy and understanding. He is at last showing signs of settling into a more stable way of life and the imposition of a Probation Order may help his progress to continue.

Case C (Crown Court)
Name: Brian Green (aged 20)
Offences: 1 Burglary
2 Theft
3 Obtain money by deception

1 Mr Green is a married man living with his wife Mary and their young son in an older-type council house in Emley. Mr and Mrs Green in fact only married on 11 December last year, although they had previously lived together for some months and have been associating on a less regular basis for about four years. Mrs Green is expecting a baby in the autumn.

2 Mr Green is a native of Emley and is the eldest of five children. His parents still live together and have an amicable relationship although they are, in fact, divorced. Mr Green retains a good relationship with his parents, whom he still visits frequently. The defendant's educational and work record have been very much interrupted by his numerous court appearances, so that he has not had the benefit of regular schooling in his home town, neither has he ever held a job .

3 With regard to his current charges Mr Green tells me that the offences were committed in order to pay household bills. As with many habitual offenders he displays little concern for the immediate victims of his actions. However he does seem to be very anxious about his present remand in custody and consequent separation from home and family.

4 Mr Green concedes that since the age of eleven he has lived most of his life in institutions. He was first taken into care in 1974 as he was committing offences and was beyond his parents' control. In subsequent years he was sent to a variety of community schools and he later served sentences of Detention Centre and Borstal Training. The records of his time in care indicate that he was sullen, unruly and lacked motivation.

5 Since he was released from an 18-month prison sentence in April 1981 he has spent the longest period out of custody for many years. He completed his period of six months licence quite well having, after an initial period of poor co-operation, reported regularly and made attempts to find employment.

6 Mr Green says that he behaved as he did for so many years because he felt that he was never properly understood or given any proper chance to improve his behaviour. He appears to be a young man who can relate to others successfully in a superficial manner. His wife tells me that he is always pleasant to her and that he only gets into trouble because he is encouraged to do so by others. Apparently he does not drink to excess and so his major difficulty would appear to be a lack of maturity and an

irresponsible attitude to life. Mr Green would say that his latest period in custody has altered him in such a way that would increase his sense of responsibility and prevent him from offending in the future.

7 Mr Green has committed a number of serious offences and is also in breach of a suspended sentence and a community service order. He realizes that he is in great danger of losing his liberty once again. He would emphasize that he now feels upset at such a prospect, when in previous years he would not have done, as he now expresses great concern for the welfare of his wife during her pregnancy and a determination to stay out of trouble. Certainly if his resolve is as strong as he maintains, he would benefit from close support, advice and guidance. However, he is aware that the court will have to decide for itself what credence to attach to his changed attitude, and that even if this is accepted a serious view will be taken of the gravity of his offences.

A reflective examination of these reports immediately raises certain comments. Some of these comments concern *omissions*: examples of this are, in cases A and C, the absence of any coherent description and analysis of the current offence or previous offending; or, in case B, the lack of any mention of the (presumably serious) previous driving offence which led to the offender being disqualified from driving at the time the report was written. Case B also has a surprising absence of pertinent social information about the domestic situation in the last three years, by comparison with the extensive discussion about earlier family upheavals.

As regards the recommendations made, Case B gives little or no indication to the bench as to why the report writer thought probation was suitable, how it would help Barry Davenport, or what being on probation would actually involve in practice; while in Case A there is, astonishingly, no mention of Mr Bishop's current financial situation, despite the fact that a fine is recommended. (This was the strongest point of criticism of any of the three reports when these cases were discussed on the RSDO courses.)

By contrast, other comments may be made about *non-relevant inclusions*. These might include some of the early domestic details in Case B; but the clearest example is in Case A, where we are entitled to ask how helpful it is to the court to be told that Mr Bishop (aged 49) played football as a boy, or that his sporting talent has been inherited by his eldest son, or that he spent most of his period of National Service in Hong Kong?

The comments made above are, of course, largely congruent with the kind of practice now being advocated in documents such as Home Office Circular 92/1986, the DHSS booklet on *Reports to Courts,* and local policy guidelines (see above). One other comment, which cannot be derived from such documents, but which anticipates one of our later arguments, is to consider how far these three reports clearly demonstrate that they have been prepared by professionally trained social workers.

While Case B comes nearest to fulfilling this criterion, it fails, as we have already noted, to indicate creative future possibilities for social work intervention within the framework of the probation order.[14] Case A has little obvious social work content, and could almost have been written by an intelligent lay person. Case C clearly indicates that the writer has a background of social work knowledge, but the use of language to distance herself from the subject of the report suggests, we would argue, that there is a lack of that true empathy which is still the cornerstone of authentic social work practice.

These criticisms – and others which could no doubt be levelled at these reports – are in one sense too easy for us to make. It is one thing to subject a report to minute analysis when removed from the bustle and pressure of daily practice; it is quite another to produce a near-perfect report in the rushed conditions of the average probation officer's or social worker's life. We have not made these criticisms to score a few points at the expense of practitioners' work. Rather the purpose has been to show how some reasonably representative 1982 reports can be called into question from the viewpoint of more recent thinking; and to introduce some ideas with which one can begin to analyse daily practice. This process is taken much further in the next two chapters, but first we want to introduce a few simple key issues which clearly affect the daily business of SIR writing.

Key issues in SIR writing

Two sets of key issues seem worth commenting on particularly at this initial stage. The first concerns what can be called *practice issues:* that is, important matters arising for the individual probation officer or social worker in preparing a report, but which nevertheless do not go to the heart of the nature of an SIR. Secondly, there are *core issues* which fundamentally address the nature and purpose of SIRs in England today.

In the category of practice issues we think that there are three key matters: time, routinization, and use of language. Each is important because in different ways it inhibits the practitioner from fully developing her professional social work skills and values in report writing.

Time was an issue which was constantly raised in the discussions on the RSDO course (see Preface). As part of the course, officers were asked to bring with them samples of their own SIR practice; in presenting and talking about these reports, it was common to hear people say that the report was not as good as they would have liked because of the shortness of the time to prepare it, and the pressure of other work at that time. This concern with the inhibiting effect of time on SIR practice has been noted by other writers. As Walker and Beaumont (1981, p.16) comment, in SIR interviews 'the probation officer has to reach a judgement quickly, often starting completely from scratch', while the reports themselves 'are often hasty judgements made under considerable pressure, on the basis of inadequate information'. And McWilliams (1986), in his in-depth research into the SIR practice of one probation team in 'Urbanshire', concluded that:

> A careful examination of the many instances in which the officers were unable to hold fast to their [expressed] professional values and beliefs in relation to the offenders about whom they were enquiring, shows one common and dominant factor and that is *time*. In almost all instances where beliefs were compromised the shortage of time was either seen as being crucial in effect, or was cited as being so by the officers concerned. (p.459)

Of course, it could be that officers, in making these claims, were sometimes using lack of time as a convenient excuse for deviations from professional values. But there is not much doubt that sometimes, at least, time acts as a real and unhelpful pressure. In respect of those 'genuine' cases, McWilliams makes the very valid point that 'time' is in fact not an independent variable, but a matter that arises from the demands of the court; it is one of the key pressures which the SIR as a court-focused document places upon the report writer.

The second practice issue we have identified is that of *routinization*. This can be related partly to the time pressures; as Walker and Beaumont (1981, p.21) put it, given the hasty nature of much report preparation, and the fact that the probation officer completes many reports, choosing recommendations from only a small range of possible sentences, 'it is not surprising that the reports emerge in a highly routinized (though sometimes idiosyncratic) conceptual form'.

Yet, probation officers on the RSDO courses did not immediately identify 'routinization' as one of their main concerns. Rather, they usually came to the courses with a degree of satisfaction about SIR practice, despite a willingness to learn more. But consideration of some theoretical issues, and close examination of some actual reports (their own and others) quite rapidly led to feelings of dissatisfaction. This developed into a view that, on reflection, SIR practice was, in many districts, in a rut, and had essentially become a matter of producing reports in a standardized manner. Some outside observers, given a batch of SIRs to read, have similarly commented upon the fact that the way the reports are presented seems to reduce the human quality and characteristics of the defendant to a flat, one-dimensional picture.

Such apparent reduction is sometimes made worse by a particular *use of language* which obscures matters, thereby hindering rather than helping the reader. The use of language in SIRs has been helpfully researched by Gail Horsley (1984). Somewhat surprisingly perhaps, her research does not reveal an over-reliance upon jargon. But it does demonstrate an over-complex use of vocabulary and syntax, to the point where many reports 'might as well be jargon, at least as far as the defendant is concerned' (p.44). It seems reasonable to speculate that such linguistic misuse occurs because of the probation officer's or social worker's desire to be seen as a professional expert; or because of a belief that the more sophisticated the language used the more impressed a bench will be; or through lack of self-confidence on the part of the report writer.

Turning to the second set of problems and dilemmas in social inquiry practice, namely the core issues, the central importance of 'realism' or 'credibility' should first be highlighted. This refers to the report writer's need, when making recommendations to the court, to ensure that they are only made within a range which the seriousness of the offence and other matters apparently permit.

The importance of this issue is widely recognized. The National Association of Probation Officers (1981), for example, said:

> It is NAPO's view that probation officers cannot entirely ignore the limitations on sentencing options imposed by the seriousness of the offence, for fear that their credibility will be damaged.

The Central Council of Probation and After-Care Committees (1981), a body composed of senior magistrates who chair probation committees, strongly stressed their view that recommendations need to be 'realistic':

> Many instances have been brought to our attention where [recommendations] may have placed false hopes in the minds of the offenders but were unrealistic in view of the nature and circumstances of the offences, the offender's past record, etc.

Probation officers and social workers who make recommendations which the bench regards as 'unrealistic' are sometimes reprimanded by magistrates or judges. One officer in McWilliams's (1986) Urbanshire study vividly recalled one instance of this:

> I have recommended a conditional discharge and he got a suspended sentence. There was a comment from the bench that this was a despicable offence, and my recommendation was totally unrealistic. The clerk even said 'My God, what have you done? Do you realize what you are talking about?', and the bench addressed me as well. (p. 470)

One important side-effect of the pressure to be realistic is, once again, its influence upon the language of reports. Recommendations arrived at in a spirit of 'realism' may well be unpalatable to the defendant, leading the report writer to wrap up the conclusion in inpenetrable language which she hopes the defendant will not understand; or to distance herself from the recommendation by a linguistic device (for example, 'the defendant recognizes the inevitability of a custodial sentence'). Indeed these linguistic forms may also appear in the earlier part of the report, leading to the unfavourable conclusion (as we consider occurs in some places in the report on Case C above).

Many probation officers and social workers clearly dislike the pressure of the need to be 'realistic', but feel obliged to go along with 'realism' because of their position within the court structure. To ignore the pressures, they feel, would betray some clients, because the officer's credibility would be diminished and therefore even in 'promising' cases the recommendation would not be followed. Often it can feel like walking a tightrope – does one give priority to the recommendation one really believes in, or to the court's expectations?

Such dilemmas are closely linked to the second core issue, that of whether the report writer is to regard herself as primarily an 'officer of the court' or as a 'social worker with offenders'? This is, of course, an old question, but one which nevertheless is still a live issue in daily practice. One aspect of the problem, for offenders over the age of 17 at least, is the existence of an apparently clear statement in the Powers of Criminal Courts Act 1973 enjoining the probation officer

> to inquire, in accordance with any directions of the court, into the circumstances or home surroundings of any person with a view to assisting the court in determining the most suitable method of dealing with his case.[15]

The phrase 'in accordance with any directions of the court' suggests that the court has the power to say what it would like included in the report, or what kind of sentence the report should especially consider.[16]

Jarvis (1980) seems to have in mind the second part of the statutory prescription in his exposition of the duty of the report writer:

> Since his purpose is not necessarily to get the offender on probation, but to help the court towards the best sentence possible, his report is intended as an essay in objectivity. The purpose is to provide the impartial professional appraisal of the offender and his situation which is vital to effective sentencing as now understood. (p. 114)

On the RSDO courses, few participants believed with Jarvis that the report could, by its very nature, be 'an essay in objectivity'; and they therefore rejected Jarvis's particular interpretation of the task of the officer of the court. But they equally acknowledged the force of the statute, and were aware that their SIR practice was therefore ultimately subject to court direction. Nevertheless, course members did not want to leave it there. They felt that the SIR should reflect aspects of their professional training as social workers. While recognizing the court's ultimate authority, they wanted the court to recognize that they themselves had certain abilities which, when used with defendants in the process of report preparation, would actually assist the court. Yet most felt that there was an uneasy juxtaposition of the two roles 'officer of the court' and 'social worker with offenders'. In daily practice this 'old chestnut' was not being resolved in any clearly thought-out way; rather, practitioners only felt able to deal with the issue in a reactive or an *ad hoc* way. We shall return to this issue in Chapter 7.

Conclusion

The issues we have raised at the end of this chapter highlight our experience that, despite official guidance, one of the hardest things for practitioners to do is to find a clear framework within which to perform one of their central tasks, whilst at the same time keeping on top of the workload. The major purpose of this book is to try to provide a coherent framework for SIR practice which can be regarded as theoretically sound, and also consistent with the official guidance of the 1980s, yet which is sufficiently robust to stand up to the difficulties and demands of day-to-day practice.

Notes

1   Taken, with slight adaptation, from McWilliams (1986, pp.489-90).

2   The others are:'because a custodial sentence is necessary for the protection of the public', and 'because the offence was so serious that a non-custodial sentence cannot be justified'. Only one of the tests need be satisfied for the court to pass a custodial sentence.

3   This provision does not apply 'if, in the circumstances of the case, the court is of the opinion that it is unnecessary to obtain a social inquiry report' (s.2(3)).

4   For juvenile offenders, a further stimulus was provided by s.23 of the 1982 Act, which inserted into s.7(7) of the Children and Young Persons Act 1969 (care orders made following criminal proceedings) criteria concerning the seriousness of the offence and the juvenile's need for care 'which he is unlikely to receive unless the court makes a care order'.

5   Sections 4A and 4B of the Powers of Criminal Courts Act 1973, inserted into that Act by Schedule 11 of the Criminal Justice Act 1982. Section 4A contains so-called 'positive' and 'negative' requirements; s.4B provides for day-centre requirements.

6   The exact wording differs slightly for the two requirements: see ss.4A(2) and 4B(2).

7   Section 3C of the Children and Young Persons Act 1969, inserted into that Act by the Criminal Justice Act 1982. This section contains three different types of requirements: supervised activities requirements; night restriction requirements; and negative requirements.

8   Actually Giller goes further, and argues, for example, that the 'social inquiry report must address [the] three different issues which define appropriateness' in s.1 (4) of the 1982 Act (see note 2 above). We disagree with this view: in our judgement, it is for the court, not the report writer, to make the final assessment about seriousness of the offence and the protection of the public, and the report writer's comments must be limited to, for example, bringing to light social information which will influence the court's assessment of the seriousness of the offence. See the fuller discussion in Chapters 2 and 4.

9   Home Office Circular 92/1986 para. 17 also suggests that reports should not be prepared 'in cases of serious and repeated offending where a custodial sentence is virtually inevitable'. This is a very contentious proposal which is discussed further in Chapter 7.

10   The draft of the 1986 Circular was more unambiguous in its disapproval of preparing reports on persons pleading not guilty. The eventual final text for Crown Court cases appears to have emerged after pressure from those concerned with workload management in the the Crown Court, who were anxious that defendants should not appear twice before that court (once for trial and once for sentence). Our own view is that, despite the workload difficulties, an unambiguous rejection of report preparation in not guilty plea cases would have been more appropriate.

11   The Demonstration Unit greatly increased the proportion of defendants placed on probation in burglary and taking and driving away cases. However, although the figures are not totally clear, it would seem from data in their report (Harraway *et al*.1985) that the team was less successful in achieving a reduction in custodial disposals.

12   This effect, known colloquially as 'up-tariffing', occurs where a report on a first-time offender recommends, for example, a supervision order, whereas without a report the court might well have imposed a fine; then on the next court appearance the court thinks that the supervision order has failed, and a more major intervention is ordered. There is some clear empirical evidence that 'up-tariffing' sometimes occurs, but the extent of it has not yet been the subject of rigorous research.

13   The cases were originally selected, for the 1982 course, by a member of the course staff who went to the central register of SIRs in his local area, and then selected from the register the first reports he came across in which the recommendations were (i) a fine, (ii) a probation order, and (iii) a recommendation for custody or an implication that

custody was the only available option. Identifying details of these and other case examples in this book have of course been altered.

14   It could be argued that, since the offence in this case was apparently not serious, no compulsory social work intervention should have been recommended. However, the available details of the case (which are only those disclosed in the report itself) are insufficient to assess whether this point is valid.

15   Powers of Criminal Courts Act 1973, schedule 3, para. 8(1). This provision replaces an identical provision previously contained in the Criminal Justice Act 1948.

16   For juveniles appearing before the court in criminal proceedings, the statutory provision is different, and appears to place the ultimate power in the hands of the local authority rather than the court: 'it shall be the duty of the [local] authority, unless they are of the opinion that it is unnecessary to do so, to make such investigations and provide the court ... with such information relating to the home surroundings, school record, health and character of the person in respect of whom the proceedings are brought *as appear to the authority likely to assist the court*' (Children and Young Persons Act 1969, s.9(1) [emphasis added]. The court may additionally request a report under s.9 (2) of the same statute, and it is the duty of the local authority to comply with this request; but this provision does not appear to give the court any power to direct how the local authority shall inquire into the case.

2 Three approaches to social inquiry reports

This chapter is about theory. We regard it as an essential part of the book because, as indicated in the Preface, getting the theory right is an essential prerequisite for good practice.

The aim of this chapter is to examine three approaches to SIR practice. The first is that advocated in the Streatfeild Report of 1961; the second, that described by various writers on what can best be called 'penal-welfare strategies'; the third, that advocated in recent years by Henri Giller and his colleagues. We have chosen these three theoretical approaches for discussion because we believe that important things can be learned from each of them – though in the case of the second theory (penal-welfare) those lessons are almost wholly negative. We hope to explain the lessons that can be learned from these approaches, and to carry those lessons forward to the rest of the book.

The Streatfeild Report
The Streatfeild Report of 1961 (Home Office and Lord Chancellor's Office 1961) was a document of immense importance in the historical development of the English SIR. It was this report which led to the great growth in the use of SIRs in the 1960s (Davies 1974).

References to the Streatfeild Report continued to be made in official guidance on SIRs as late as the Home Office Circular 17/1983 (discussed in Chapter 1). But by then most probation officers and social workers had long since ceased to read Streatfeild, or to realize that it contained a worthwhile discussion of the theoretical rationale for SIR practice. Two writers who did realize this, however, were Curran and Chambers (1982, p.34) who, despite some criticisms of Streatfeild, argued that the report still then offered – 20 years after first publication – the clearest guidance available on the theoretical rationale for the structure and contents of the SIR. We agree with their view, and therefore a brief re-examination of Streatfeild's ideas will form a valuable introduction to our own approach to SIR practice.

Sentencing: backward-looking and forward-looking considerations
Streatfeild's starting-point was that of a perceived change in the nature of sentencing. 'Sentencing used to be a comparatively simple matter', the committee said:

> The primary objective was to fix a sentence proportionate to the offender's culpability, and the system has been loosely described as the 'tariff system'. The facts of the offence and the offender's record were the main pieces of information needed by the court, and the defence could bring to notice any mitigating circumstances. (para. 257)

In such a sentencing system, not very complex procedures were necessary for obtaining information relevant to the sentence: 'the information was about past events which could normally be reliably described; and it was readily available' (para. 257).

Increasingly, however, the committee felt, courts were now trying to influence future events as well as to look back at the current offence and the past record. In talking about 'influencing future events', the committee had in mind especially considerations of reforming the offender (or, sometimes, individually deterring him), though they also noted that general deterrence and the future protection of the public were other sentencing aims which in some ways were concerned with future events. Given that courts were now attempting these difficult future-oriented goals, a different kind of information needed to be placed before them:

> The information which enabled the court to assess culpability is not necessarily the information which indicates how the offender should be reformed, much less how potential offenders should be deterred. (para. 263)

This new kind of information, the committee thought, should be of two kinds. The first kind was *general*, and suggested that appropriate research results should be communicated to sentencers on a regular basis (there is a notably optimistic paragraph on prediction studies at this point (para. 278)). The second kind of new information, of more relevance to this book, was *individual*, that is, information about individual offenders. As regards such information, the committee enunciated as a 'cardinal principle' the view that:

> a sentence should be based on *comprehensive* and *reliable* information which is *relevant* to the objectives in the court's mind'. (para. 323, see also para. 292) [emphasis added]

The committee's emphasis here is not just on reliability of information about individuals (the court should be able to trust the information it is given), and on comprehensiveness (a full picture should be presented). There is an additional strand, that of relevance, which can sharply qualify the apparent width of the 'comprehensiveness' requirement:

> Information should not be proliferated for information's sake. It is not simply a matter of providing the courts with the fullest possible information about offenders. A mass of background information can be collected with comparative ease, but irrelevant information is not only useless but possibly harmful. There is a risk that it may cloud the issue before the court and induce a cosy feeling in which the absence of really useful information passes unnoticed. The test to be applied is whether the information can help the court to reach a better decision. (para. 293)

Social inquiry reports – three specific tasks

What then, according to Streatfeild, is relevant social information to be presented to a court in an SIR? The committee was extremely explicit on this point; it said that an SIR can 'helpfully and properly' supply the court with three (but only three) relevant kinds of information:

> (a)   information about the social and domestic background of the offender which is relevant to the court's assessment of his culpability;
> (b)   information about the offender and his surroundings which is relevant to the court's consideration of how his criminal career might be checked; and
> (c)   an opinion as to the likely effect on the offender's criminal career of probation or some other specified form of sentence. (para. 335)

The clear implication is that other information provided for the court (that is, anything not specifically coming within one of the three formulae spelled out in para. 335) is irrelevant information, and not to be included. This is a crucial point which was often not appreciated by subsequent practitioners and writers about SIRs. For example, in his famous text on SIRs, Perry (1974, p.43) comments that he 'did not find any reason for the exclusion [in a minority of cases] of the basic facts about the subject, such as where he was born and the number of other children in the family' – yet place of birth and number of siblings are surely often likely to constitute irrelevant information, in Streatfeild's terminology, especially in an adult sample such as the one Perry was examining.

Many probation officers and social workers seem not to have been trained specifically in SIR writing in their social work qualifying courses, despite the central importance of SIR preparation in criminal-justice-based social work.   In the absence of such specific training, it seems that officers have tended to treat the first three-quarters of a social inquiry report as something of a *social history,* and they have tried to apply the techniques they have been taught about social-history-gathering to this task (see McWilliams 1986, pp.424-8).[1]   Yet the message of Streatfeild, which we would strongly endorse, was that SIR preparation and writing is not just a matter of social-history-gathering; rather, the task is that of preparing and presenting a report which will be relevant in relation to certain specific objectives.

A second point to notice from the three sub-sections of Streatfeild's para. 335 (see above) is the distinction between the first and second categories, (a) and (b). As Streatfeild pointed out at the time it reported, SIRs tended to include, in respect of these categories, a variety of matters such as home surroundings, family background, school and work record, spare-time activities, attitude to the offence, etc. Usually, the committee went on, 'categories (a) and (b) in paragraph 335 are at present treated as one ' (para. 336). Nevertheless, it suggested, it was 'important to recognize the distinction'. We strongly agree that it is necessary to recognize this distinction, and we build on it in this book, albeit in a somewhat different context (see Chapters 4 and 5).

Can Streatfeild's three tasks be supported today?
We have shown that, for Streatfeild, there were three specific and separable tasks to be accomplished within the ambit of SIR writing. Can these three specific tasks be supported in the same terms today?

(a)   *Information relevant to culpability.* Little time need be spent on this heading. All commentators, from very different schools of thought, seem to agree that report writers should furnish courts with social information relevant to culpability (see Chapter 1 for some views of this kind). We also agree with this opinion, and need to say no more about it now, though we elaborate it in Chapter 4.

(b)   *Information relevant to the court's consideration of how the defendant's criminal career may be checked.* This is a much more difficult objective to support in the modern context. As is well known, at the time of the Streatfeild Report there was great optimism about 'penal treatments', and a hope that researchers would soon be able to identify with confidence certain treatments which would check criminal careers, even those of some hardened recidivists. That hope has proved largely illusory. Although not all penal treatments have failed in preventing recividism, the hopeful results from treatment research are rather fragmentary, and it is very difficult even for the specialist researcher to offer more than the odd glimmer of hope here and there that this or that treatment might succeed in preventing re-offending (see Brody 1976; Walker 1985, Ch. 6). For the report writer faced with an individual client, the only really safe rule is to say that, for a given individual, little or nothing can be said to the court along the lines that 'action X will definitely help to check D's criminal career' or 'action Y will definitely hinder D's rehabilitation'.

Although it is important to give full recognition to this radical change in the penological scene since the time of the Streatfeild Report, it does not necessarily follow that the thinking of the Streatfeild Committee, in distinguishing categories (a) and (b), needs to be completely abandoned in the modern context. Streatfeild's principal distinction, in relation to categories (a) and (b), was that category (a) (culpability) related to past events, whereas category (b) was about influencing future events (see above). If one returns to that kind of thinking, and ignores the specific wording of para. 335(b), it becomes possible to produce a revised formulation, as follows:

(a) information about the social background of the offender which is relevant to the court's assessment of his culpability (backward-looking);
(b) information about the social background and the present situation of the offender which is relevant to some consideration of his future prospects (forward-looking).

To elaborate this formulation a little, the point is that for all human subjects (offenders or not) it is generally possible to adduce some evidence or information about their current circumstances, lifestyle, approach to decision-making, etc. which is relevant to a consideration of their future prospects. (Anyone who has ever been a parent of a young adult should recognize this point very readily.) It follows that this may therefore remain a valid category of SIR information even in a context where producing information 'relevant to how a criminal career may be checked' is in a specific sense impossible. In this book, it will be argued that, so formulated, this does remain a valid category for SIR writing. This point is returned to in Chapter 5.

(c) *An opinion as to the likely effect on the offender's criminal career of probation or some other specified form of sentence.* Much the same comments apply here as in (b). The report writer is unlikely to be able to provide an opinion in quite the terms proposed by Streatfeild, in view of the somewhat depressing results of treatment research as regards the reduction of re-offending. Nevertheless, there is no reason why in a more general sense the report writer should not write about, for example, the offender's possible future prospects in such a way as to include the likelihood of co-operation on a community service order, or on probation with a specifically worked-out plan for what is to be achieved under supervision, etc.; in short, to write intelligently about future possibilities relevant to several sentencing options before the court.

This is, again, a matter to which more specific attention is given later (see Chapter 6), and it is at that point that mention is made of the celebrated controversy, arising from this part of the Streatfeild Report, about whether 'recommendations', 'opinions', or something else should be made to the court by the report writer.[2] At this point in our discussion we simply want to note one very important part of Streatfeild's argument as it was applied to this third category of relevant information in an SIR. The report writer's opinions, said Streatfeild:

> relate to only one of the possible considerations in the court's mind: how to stop the offender from offending again. The court has still to consider the nature of the offence and the public interest, and *it has the sole responsibility for the sentence which is ultimately passed. The probation officer should never give his opinion in a form which suggests that it relates to all the considerations in the court's mind* ... [the opinion is] proferred for the assistance of the court on one aspect of the question before it. Provided that this is understood by all concerned, there can be no grounds for thinking that in expressing a frank opinion on the likely effect on the offender of probation or other forms of sentence the probation officer is in any way usurping the functions of the court. (para. 346) [emphasis added]

In the modern context, this passage again has to be re-cast. In offering views about likely sentences the report writer is unable to say anything very specific about 'how to stop the offender from offending again', as Streatfeild put it, but she may nevertheless be able to say valuable things about likely sentencing options. In doing so, however, Streatfeild was surely right to insist that the report writer cannot and should not cover 'all the considerations in the court's mind' – including general deterrence, the protection of the public, how the seriousness of a particular offence is to be weighed, etc. Probation officers and social workers do not have the training or experience to consider such matters fully, nor is there any reason for them to do so, since the court has a duty to consider the relevance of issues of this kind, and it is 'the court ... [which] has the sole responsibility for the sentence which is ultimately passed'.[3] The job of the report writer is an important one, but it does indeed relate to only some aspects of the court's task. This is an important point which has been too often neglected by probation officers, social workers, and those writing about social inquiry reports.[4] As Streatfeild noted, a firm appreciation of this point should make any observer realize that in commenting on sentence the report writer is not 'in any way usurping the functions of the court'. Equally, an understanding of this point leads some way towards a solution of the realism/credibility dilemma which was raised in Chapter 1. These matters will be returned to later in the book.

Streatfeild, 'scientism' and subsequent research and theorization
It has been noted that Curran and Chambers (1982, p. 34) thought that the Streatfeild Report still offered, in the early 1980s, the clearest guidance as a theoretical framework for writing SIRs. Curran and Chambers were not, however, blind to Streatfeild's deficiencies:

> Unfortunately, that guidance was based upon a specific philosophy of science which viewed the achievements of the social sciences as accumulative. It is not a sufficient response simply to see the 'failure of treatment' literature ... as a temporary set-back. Both the Home Office Research Unit and the Probation Service would seem to be seeking for a new direction away from the so-called treatment model of rehabilitation.

We agree with this comment. Streatfeild's view of the application of social science to sentencing was extremely optimistic, somewhat deterministic, and firmly of the view that the research achievements of the coming years would be accumulative. In short, Streatfeild had a 'scientistic' approach. Over the years, the negative results of treatment researches, and theoretical critiques of rehabilitation (for a summary, see Bottoms 1980) have led many to be more pessimistic. Thus, for example, Lady Wootton, a member of the Streatfeild Committee, writing in 1981 and looking back to her views at the time of the Streatfeild Report, commented:

My final (Hamlyn) lecture ended on a relatively optimistic note, still cherishing the hope ... that more refined methods of investigation, together with the rapid growth of electronic mechanisms for handling more complex data, may make sentencers better aware of their own decisions, and more competent to achieve whatever it is they want to achieve. But I have to confess that over the years since these lectures were delivered, I have been increasingly haunted by the image ... of the whole penal system as in a sense a gigantic irrelevance – wholly misconceived as a method of controlling phenomena the origins of which are inextricably rooted in the structure of our society. (p.119)

Hence, neither sentencers nor report writers can now talk confidently, as the Streatfeild Report did, of 'seeking to *control* future events' (para. 269), [emphasis added], or of information definitely *relevant* to 'how the defendant's criminal career may be checked'. As Curran and Chambers say, we have to take this change very seriously, and not assume that it is a merely temporary phenomenon. And if we still wish to use some of the frameworks of the Streatfeild Report (as this book does), then these have to be recast in this new context. That task we have begun in this chapter in our comments on Streatfeild's paragraphs 335(b) and 335 (c); it is a task which will be continued throughout the book.

The SIR and penal-welfare strategies

The second theoretical approach to be considered demands some understanding of history. Historically, the SIR in this country can be seen as very much the product of what David Garland (1985) has described as the new 'penal-welfare strategies' of early 20th century Britain. To appreciate this more fully, it is necessary to understand these 'penal-welfare strategies' in outline.

As Garland has shown, the penal system in England in the second half of the 19th century operated primarily within a framework of legal justice:

Offenders were to be accorded their just desserts in the form of a proportional measure of retribution. However, it was well-established that the question of proportion and dessert must be considered along with the question of deterrence, since justice partakes of social prudence as well as the natural order. Consequently this framework of justice ... promoted the twin goals of deterrence and retribution. These two terms appear again and again throughout all the representations of penality in the nineteenth century. (p.16)

Within a few years at the beginning of this century, much of this was changed, or at any rate supplemented, by a range of new measures such as probation orders and borstal training; and, for example, the juvenile court was also created at this time. *Individualization*, a concept foreign to Victorian penality, became an important new approach in penology. Deterrence and retribution remained, but, in the new system:

> Criminals are presented as individuals to be pitied, cared for and, if possible, reclaimed. Whenever apparently punitive or deterrent measures are under discussion, they appear as last resorts when all else has failed, as unpleasant but unavoidable evils, out of keeping with the general tenor of the system. (Garland 1985, p.27)

The new individualized approach contained three different kinds of penal strategy – described by Garland as the *normalizing sector* (probation, after-care, etc.), the *corrective sector* (institutional training: borstals, reformatories, etc.), and the *segregative sector* (preventive detention, etc., for those who have been recalcitrant when other approaches have been applied). The strategies in the normalizing sector – those of most relevance to this book – were:

> concerned not just to prevent law-breaking, but also to inculcate specific norms and attitudes. By means of the personal influence of the probation or after-care officer, they attempt to straighten out characters and to reform the personality of their clients in accordance with the requirements of 'good citizenship'. (Garland 1985, p. 238)

Thus, the whole thrust of the new kind of penalty born in this period – which inserts welfare and individualization into the penal apparatus, in a set of penal-welfare strategies – is, in a way, to transform the nature of law:

> [This does] not mean to say that the law fades into the background or that the institutions of justice tend to disappear, but rather that the law operates *more and more as a norm,* and that the judicial institution is increasingly incorporated into a continuum of apparatuses (medical, administrative, and so on) whose functions are for the most part regulatory. (Foucault 1981, p.144) [emphasis added]

Various writers interested in penal-welfare strategies have focused on the SIR – and on other social inquiries in other parts of the penal and welfare systems of the modern State – as a key element in this system: for the social inquiry helps, *inter alia,* to sort the deserving from the undeserving as potential recipients of welfare or benevolence.

Thus Foucault (1977, pp.184-94)[5], in a celebrated chapter on the means of correct training, speaks of 'the examination' (or inquiry) as combining the techniques of *hierarchical observation* and of *normalizing judgements*. By 'hierarchical observation' he means methods of surveillance exercised by a powerful person or institution upon those in a lower position in the social hierarchy; by 'normalizing judgements' he means judgements made by social agents with a view to maximizing the power of social norms. So the examination is:

> A normalizing gaze, a surveillance that makes it possible to qualify, to classify and to punish. It establishes over individuals a visibility through which one differentiates them and judges them ... In it are combined the ceremony of power and the form of the experiment, the deployment of force and the establishment of truth. (Foucault 1977, p.184)

An example of social inquiry practice carried out very much in this style – though in the specific field of investigating families seeking public assistance, rather than for a court report – is given in a book by Jacques Donzelot (1980, pp.122-5). Donzelot quotes a French article on 'social inquiry', written in 1920; the article proposes that before meeting the family the investigator should gather all existing material from administrative files, and then approach several other people, 'in order to get a clear notion of the life of the family itself' – these people include the teacher, the father's employer, the landlord, the concierge, the neighbours, and the local shopkeepers (except perhaps the local wine merchant, 'who should always be treated with suspicion'!). Thereafter the investigator, armed with all this information should visit the home – though always without prior appointment.[6] The first visit should be in the middle of the afternoon, in order to catch the mother at home alone. A subsequent evening visit then allows father to be questioned, and his evidence tested against his wife's. During these visits various ways of verifying the family way of life are recommended, including a close examination of the dwelling and its furniture; it is even, as Donzelot comments, 'not considered inappropriate to raise the lids of a few cooking pots, to examine food stocks and bedding, and if need be, to take a few telling photographs'. The visits, however, are not to be conducted in a hostile manner, but pleasantly; they should 'give rise to as much talk, back and forth, as possible – these conversations always give pleasure to the persons one is questioning'(!).

This example is an extreme one, and it comes, of course, from a very different cultural and administrative context from the one we are concerned with in this book. Nevertheless, some glimpses of not dissimilar practices and attitudes can be found in some older SIRs for the courts in England. For example, among a sample of 1940s reports which have been made available to us, one contains the following description of the home:

> The rooms appeared to be untidy when I saw them, but the man had only just got up and the breakfast things had not been cleared away. The walls were dirty and smeared with dirty fingerprints, and the room generally bore an unclean aspect. There was a smell of washing about the place. The sleeping arrangements leave much to be desired.

In a different vein, but in the same investigatory style, another report was written on a man aged 27 charged on three counts of obtaining by false pretences. The man (who we may call Mr Black) lived at home with his widowed mother, and claimed that his offences were committed through anxiety and lack of self-control brought on by the frequent presence in the house of a Mr Brown, a sergeant in the Special Constabulary. The report writer comments:

> The mother denies that anything happens in the home to cause her son worry but I understand, *from enquiries I have made,* that Mr Brown is a frequent visitor, and that local opinion is (without any real evidence) that his visits are of an amorous nature. [emphasis added]

As for Mr Black himself, the report described his character in the Armed Services (from which he was discharged after war service two years previously) as 'exemplary', and his subsequent employment record as 'good'; yet the report writer concluded, on wholly unspecified grounds, that 'in my opinion this man is either abnormal and in need of treatment, or alternatively he is an excellent actor and liar'.

We have included this material for a definite reason. It is, we think, important for present-day practitioners of the SIR to understand: first, that the SIR owes its origins to a particular phase of penal history, the birth of the penal-welfare strategies; secondly, that, within those strategies, the idea of social inquiry (in the broad sense) played a key part, and was carried out by combining the techniques of hierarchical observation and normalizing judgement; and thirdly, that SIR practice consistent with these precepts has been carried out in England in the past.

When these points are grasped, the obvious questions remain: to what extent is social inquiry practice still conducted in this manner, and should it be?

Our answers to these questions are as follows. First, we believe that Foucault was right to describe social inquiry as a mixture of hierarchical observation and normalizing judgement. Given the fact that the report writer has much more power than the offender, the social inquiry situation is inevitably 'hierarchical' to an extent; and the moral frameworks which the officer (who is, after all, an officer of the court) brings to her task will inevitably involve an element of 'normalizing judgement' in the interviewing and the report writing. But secondly, there are very different ways of carrying out tasks which necessarily involve hierarchical observation and normalizing judgement. The repellent procedures recommended in the practice manual quoted by Donzelot (1980) are one version of what (for simplicity) can be called the 'hierarchical examination'; what goes on in probation offices and social work departments all over the country is another, much milder version. To anticipate the argument of the next chapter, we believe that r*espect for persons* and *care for persons* are core social work values, and that a serious adherence to such values (which we firmly advocate) involves a conscious effort to minimize the 'hierarchical examination' tradition of social inquiry, even though that tradition cannot (in the nature of the inquiry) be completely eliminated. To take a simple practical example of what this approach means in practice, we believe that the report writer should never (except in emergencies) attempt the 'surprise visit' to the home without prior appointment, but should show respect for the subject of the inquiry by giving him prior notice of her approach.

Thus the lessons that can be learned from considering the social inquiry as 'hierarchical examination' are almost wholly negative lessons; but the lessons are both very important, and, in some ways, very practical.

The work of Henri Giller and his colleagues

The third theoretical approach that we want to consider is much more recent. In an influential recorded tape on SIRs, Tutt and Giller (1984) range across a number of issues. On side one of the tape, Norman Tutt discusses some aspects of the legal background to SIRs, some aspects of psychological theory relevant to SIRs, and some research findings from the Centre for Youth, Crime and Community at Lancaster University. On side two of the tape, Henri Giller discusses the Criminal Justice Act 1982, and then outlines a 'blueprint for action ... which seeks to acknowledge criticisms and deficiencies in existing practice'. In a subsequent book written with Allison Morris (Morris and Giller 1987, pp.218-28), Giller uses a similar framework of analysis, and offers additional research evidence, but (it being a different kind of text) the 'blueprint for action' is less prominent.

We wish to concentrate attention here on Giller's very interesting 'blueprint for action' which seems to have three interlinked theoretical sources. First, it draws upon Norman Tutt's analysis of the psychological literature, in which he emphasizes that individuals' behaviour is often situation-specific rather than explicable in terms of enduring personality traits.[7] Secondly, it draws upon labelling theory,[8] and takes the view that often 'it is the failure of the services through which ... children proceed at an earlier stage which determines their eventual designation as difficult, disruptive, and the like'; moreover, 'the social inquiry report writing process contributes substantially to this'. Thirdly, it draws upon recent critiques of rehabilitative treatment in penology (see the earlier discussion).

There are three particular aspects of Giller's blueprint which we think it is useful to discuss here: the first two relate to the individual report writer's practice, and the last to wider aspects of the SIR.[9]

Social work reports?
First, Giller makes the very challenging assertion that 'social inquiry reports are not a social work document'. What does he mean by this?

Positively, Giller wants to emphasize that SIRs are written for courts, 'to determine what should happen to [an] offender as a consequence of the commission of a proved offence'. The SIR, then, is 'a document with a specific purpose for a limited exercise'.
Negatively, Giller is very anxious to avoid the practice whereby, all too often, SIRs have been written by practitioners as a form of social history (see above, p.24). So, he emphasizes, SIRs 'are not the genealogy of the child, or of the child's parents, or of the parents' parents'. Moreover, he is very anxious to avoid social information being presented as 'a freefloating catalogue of pathology', for, given the emphasis on labelling theory:

> Without the links, without the connections, between this background information and the reason for the [court] appearance being made, the writer leaves open the possibility of the offender being doubly jeopardised: once by the misconduct, and once by the pathology.

As should be clear from our earlier discussion of Streatfeild's approach, we agree with much of this, though we would place rather less stress than Giller on labelling theory.[10] But does any of this, even in Giller's own terms, imply that the SIR is 'not a social work document'?

It is important to emphasize that Henri Giller is not hostile to social work as such. On the contrary, he hopes that his blueprint for SIR practice in the juvenile courts will:

> hopefully halt and eventually reverse the trend ... whereby the influence of the social work professions in juvenile justice systems and the opportunity to participate in and practise social work with delinquent adolescents has been steadily contracting.

Giller then advocates a strategy for SIR writing very similar to that first proposed by Peter Raynor (1980), based on (in Giller's words) 'the context of culpability and the realistic alternative sentence'; and he concludes that:

> While it can be argued that the approach we have advocated here is not the social worker's job, unless these issues are challenged and strategies such as these adopted, the prospect of being able to actually do social work with offenders will further decline ... *This would be a loss to both the juvenile justice system and to juvenile offenders.* [emphasis added]

Raynor's work will be discussed in subsequent chapters. Suffice it to say here that we certainly do not regard Raynor's article as proposing the abolition of the SIR as a social work document (and neither, we are sure, would he). We think that Giller, in his justifiable wish to press for specificity in the SIR, and his equally laudable wish to abandon the 'social history' approach to SIR writing, has mistakenly assumed that a 'social work' approach necessarily means a social history approach. In the following chapter, we present the alternative view that the SIR emphatically is a social work document, though in no way do we wish to resurrect or to defend either the 'social history' or the 'free-floating pathology' approach to SIR practice rightly rejected by Giller.

Aiming at the least restrictive sanction?
As part of his argument for SIRs based on 'the context of culpability and the realistic alternative sentence', Giller proposes that:

> the overriding principle of report writing should be to aim at the least restrictive sanction in keeping with the severity of the offence.

This principle arises from something like the following argument.

First, the least powerful groups in society run a disproportionate risk of being involved in the formal criminal justice system. Secondly, they are then sometimes further discriminated against by 'the inculpatory nature of much of the material currently presented in social inquiry reports'. If social work intervention with such offenders could be shown to be beneficial, then 'such discrimination might be seen as positive'; but frequently this cannot be shown, and all that occurs is a more intrusive intervention into the child's life than would be justified on the basis of the criminal conduct alone. Therefore, the least restrictive alternative is best for the offender: it is in his current interests to receive as minimal a sentence as possible, and a more intrusive sentence this time may well encourage the courts to pass an even heavier sentence on the next court appearance, if there is one.[11]

Attractive as this argument sounds, it contains a serious difficulty. Throughout his argument, Giller assumes that it is legitimate for the social worker presenting an SIR to consider in the report all the issues before the court, including the protection of the public and the seriousness of the offence. As we have seen in the discussion of the Streatfeild Report, above, this is a view which, at the end of the day, simply cannot be sustained, because of the report writer's structural position *vis-à-vis* the sentencer. It also follows from that structural position that the report writer cannot coherently argue for the least restrictive alternative, because the report writer is not in a position to develop arguments which relate to all the factors which may be weighed by the court.

A further difficulty with Giller's approach is that it makes the SIR in effect indistinguishable from the defence lawyer's plea of mitigation (except that it comes from a different source, and from a person with a different kind of training): both can be expected to plead for the lowest possible sentence. Quite apart, then, from the theoretical difficulties in arguing for the task of the SIR as being to present the least restrictive alternative (see above), it is probably the case that if and when a court realizes that a social worker or probation officer is routinely engaged in what are in effect pleas of mitigation, there is a serious danger of losing legitimacy in the court's eyes.

Three levels of analysis

The final aspect of Giller's analysis that we wish to highlight is his clear differentiation between three levels of analysis in thinking about SIRs. The first of these three levels is the *individual report writer's practice*, about which no more need be said here. Secondly, there is the *organizational context* (within the report writer's own agency): this includes such issues as the 'monitoring' or 'gatekeeping' of reports, and agency decisions about the kind of cases in which pre-trial SIRs should be prepared. Thirdly, and finally, there is the *systems context* (relating to aspects of the criminal justice system beyond the report writer's own agency). Giller explains the relevance of this systems context in the following way:

> The strategies I have discussed will have a limited impact unless they are understood and appreciated by those who make the final decision within the juvenile court. Obviously, therefore, approaches need to be made to the juvenile court magistrates, to justices' clerks, to the police and to the local education services, so that some locally negotiated strategy on report- writing presentation is understood and agreed by all the participating parties.

We believe that this three-level method of analysis is extremely helpful. This book is primarily about the preparation of individual reports (a subject well worth attention in its own right), but Giller's very clear three-level analysis most usefully reminds us of other important dimensions of SIR practice. These other dimensions, and some of Giller's specific suggestions in respect of them, will be discussed in Chapter 7.

Conclusion

By analyzing, in this chapter, three theoretical approaches to SIR practice, we have begun to hint at some aspects of the kind of practice we would recommend; and, in particular, we have indicated our points of disagreement with the three approaches outlined. Amongst other things, we have made clear that for us the SIR is a social work document. In the next chapter, we must argue more positively for that position, and spell out a little of what it means.

Notes

1   So, for example, one probation officer spoke of how the preparation of general social histories as a student 'had an influence on the way my inquiry reports are written', and added that, when preparing SIRs, 'in social work terms it's better just to sit there and prepare a non-directive social history' (McWilliams 1986, pp.424-5).

2   The Streatfeild Report advocated the avoidance of the term 'recommendation', since this word suggests that it relates to all the considerations in the court's mind. But in subsequent years, 'recommendation' quickly acquired a universal currency (see Ford 1972, p.10; Harris 1979).

3   It is important to emphasize, however, that report writers can and should provide the courts with information relevant to offending and culpability (see Chapters 1 and 4) and that this information may affect the court's judgement concerning, for example,

the seriousness of the offence or the need for general deterrence.

4   The issue is, however, strongly emphasized in the 1987 DHSS booklet *Reports to Courts* (DHSS 1987, paras 23-6, 99-101, 122-4). See also Home Office Circular 92/1986, para. 13.

5   Foucault (1977) and Garland (1985) disagree on certain key points in their respective analyses, but it is not necessary to pursue these issues here.

6   It is worth noting in this regard the remarks of a Mr Williamson, an English probation officer, who in 1908 said: 'Someone may ask, when do you visit your cases? And in replying I would inform then that I have no fixed time, but give surprise visits, morning, noon and night' (quoted in Garland 1985, p.263).

7   This is an important debate in contemporary criminology more generally: for an introduction see Heal and Laycock (1986), especially the chapters by Cornish and Clarke and by Trasler.

8   Labelling theory emphasizes the impact of societal reactions to deviance upon the person labelled as deviant; and, in particular, it postulates the possibility of deviance amplification occurring as a result of societal interventions.

9   It should be noted that Giller's discussion is, throughout, restricted to juvenile offenders, but the principles he is outlining do not seem to be specific to offenders in the juvenile age-range.

10 For a useful survey of labelling theory see Plummer (1979); *inter alia,* he argues that 'although it is true that to date labelling theory has not usually fared well at the hands of empirical researchers, this is largely due to the narrow interpretation given to the theory by the researchers' (p.118).

11 This is the phenomenon known as 'up-tariffing': see Chapter 1, note 12.

3 Social work reports

In the course of his analysis of SIRs (see Chapter 2), Henri Giller raised what he called the 'seemingly simple, but often neglected question: for whom are social inquiry reports written?' (Tutt and Giller 1984). Giller's answer to this question is clear and straightforward:

> social inquiry reports are written for ... courts to determine what should happen to [an] offender as a consequence of the commission of a proved offence.

A careful consideration of this simple question, therefore, ensures an appropriate recognition of the point that SIRs should be focused documents, 'with a specific purpose for a limited exercise' as Giller rightly puts it.[1]

But there is another simple question which also needs to be asked; it is the counterpart of the first question. This second question is: *by whom are social inquiry reports written?* Only by exploring the answer to this question, in conjunction with the answer to the first question, can a balanced view of desirable SIR practice be developed.

One of the great merits of the Streatfeild Report – though one often now forgotten – is that in the major chapter on information relating to individual offenders (Chapter 11) the committee took great pains to enumerate a variety of sources from whom the court may receive information about defendants – the prosecution, the police, the probation service, the prison authorities, the medical profession, and so on. The importance of keeping in mind the unique perspective of each of these sources was emphasized. At the end of the chapter, the committee expressly rejected a suggestion that one person should be responsible for co-ordinating all the information and presenting it in a kind of digest for the court; for, the committee argued:

> In general it is preferable that the different reports should be separately submitted so that the court can bear in mind the different approaches of the services responsible for them: a probation report is necessarily made from a different angle from a prison governor's report. At present

no one service has the necessary knowledge and experience to be able to report itself on all aspects of the case on which the court needs information. (para. 429)

The last sentence is as true today as it was in 1961.The necessary implication, which complements some of the other points made in the Streatfeild Report (see Chapter 2), is that we should not expect an SIR to contain all the information which a court needs to consider in reaching a balanced sentencing decision. Rather, just as a court will expect a doctor's report to be written in a way which reflects appropriate medical knowledge, experience, and values, so a court should recognize that an SIR also reflects the writer's particular knowledge, experience and values. In the case of the SIR, of course, the essential point is that the report (whether prepared by a probation officer or local authority social worker) will be written *by a person trained in social work.*

We believe that a careful consideration of the implications of this simple point leads to a clearer understanding of what is involved in the professional task of preparing and writing SIRs.

Social work knowledge, skills and values
What, then, are the distinctive features of a court report written by a person trained in social work? In a nutshell, we would argue that such a report should reflect social work knowledge and experience, social work skills and social work values. Each of these elements must briefly be considered.[2]

By *social work knowledge and experience* we do not mean any one particular academic discipline, but rather a combination of some understanding of the social sciences; a knowledge of relevant law, procedures and agency functions; experience of the local community in various aspects; and an understanding of interpersonal dynamics. These, and other areas of relevant knowledge, are discussed in standard social work texts (for example, Davies 1985), and they do not require elaboration here.[3] We would, however, want to insist that an SIR should always reflect the fact that it has been prepared with social work knowledge. Yet this is not always achieved in practice: for example, in Chapter 1 it was seen how one report (Case A, p.9) could probably have been written by an intelligent lay-person untrained in social work.

Turning, secondly, to *social work skills*, these have been identified by Martin Davies (1985, pp.223-4) as including:

adeptness in assessment and decision-making, confidence in human relationships, the demonstration of sensitivity to the client, ability to influence people in positions of power, fluency in report-writing, flexible and
practical responsiveness to volatile social circumstances, ability to give
appropriate help in a wide variety of situations, and awareness of
treatment strategies that meet the client's needs.

Some items on this list are no doubt controversial, but many would
gain widespread acceptance among social workers. However, the
list is undoubtedly of a very general kind. Like others, we believe
that many social work skills are best understood when they are seen
in action in relation to specific tasks or duties, and, further, that there
are some particular skills which are called for in preparing and
writing an SIR. But since it is difficult to say much about these skills
unless and until we are clearer about the specific *content* of an SIR,
no more will be said about social work skills at this point. We hope,
instead, that the nature of these skills will become apparent in the
next three chapters, which deal with different aspects of the content
of SIRs.

Social work knowledge and social work skills are both extremely
important components of SIR practice. But taken by themselves they
are incomplete. An exclusive emphasis upon them can lead to a
dangerous reliance on procedure and technique as ends in themselves, without reference to deeper purposes or values; and indeed,
as Michael Whan (1986, p.249) puts it: 'in many areas of human life,
technique has become the dominant response and ideology'. In order
to counteract this danger, we would argue that social work skills and
social work knowledge should always be used in a way which is congruent with *social work values*. This means that, ultimately, social
work should be seen as a form of 'practical moral engagement', as
Whan (p.243) has put it.

But what *are* 'social work values'? In considering this question,
the work of Martin Davies again provides a helpful starting point.
According to Davies (1985, p.234):

> The social work tradition that has evolved over ninety years decrees that
> welfare functions in respect of the elderly, the handicapped, the deviant
> and the deprived shall be fulfilled in a manner that respects the individu-
> ality of those involved, and always recognises potential for survival and
> growth, and that reflects an absolute commitment to care.

The threefold value-position which Davies here attributes to social work cannot, we think, be subscribed to in full. In particular, the notion of 'absolute commitment to care' embodies an unrealistic idealism and a failure to address possibilities of conflict of interest. Nevertheless, somewhat reformulated, Davies's three core values of social work have much strength. We would reformulate them as follows:

(a) *Respect for persons.* Davies's 'respect [for] the individuality of those involved' is best formulated as the simple but profound concept of 'respect for persons'.[4] By respect for persons we mean, as Dworkin (1977, p.272) puts it, treating social work clients as 'human beings who are capable of forming and acting on intelligent conceptions of how their lives should be lived'.[5]

(b) *Care for persons.* Whilst Davies's 'absolute commitment to care' is too strong, there is no doubt that the social work profession must sustain a caring approach towards its clients, again best encapsulated in the simple concept of 'care for persons'. It is important to notice that 'respect for persons' and 'care for persons' are not the same thing: indeed, one without the other is inadequate. For example, a social work practice strongly committed to caring, but which does not respect its clients, can become a benevolent tyranny as people are shuffled off into old people's homes 'in their own interests' but without consulting them; or, in the crime field, are 'sentenced to social work' (see Bryant *et al.* 1978). Conversely, a social work practice which makes a point of respecting persons and their choices, but which does not offer care, is ultimately only an abstraction devoid of human commitment and compassion.

(c) *Hope for the future and recognition of clients' potential for survival and growth.* 'Respect for persons' and 'care for persons' are static concepts: that is, they are about how a social worker should deal with her client(s) at a given moment in time. They say nothing in themselves about future possibilities. Yet social work at its best has always contained another dimension, a future dimension which sees hope and possibilities even in the most apparently unlikely individuals and social situations. This is what Davies refers to in his comment that social work 'recognizes potential for survival and growth'; we have incorporated his phrase in our formulation, whilst prefacing it with what we would regard as the more powerful and general concept of 'hope for the future'.[6]

The quotation from Martin Davies which we have used as a starting-point for this discussion of social work values seems to imply that the 90-year-old development of social work has been constant in its adherence to the three identified core values. Davies thus seems to want both to assert the importance of the core values, and to say that they have always been at the heart of social work since its inception. We think it is important to say, however, that these are two very different issues, which should be carefully distinguished.

The three core values of respect for persons, care for persons, and hope for the future are clearly normative principles. We hope they will attract widespread support and acceptance among our readers as being in a real way fundamental to social work practice, but their substantiation cannot of course depend simply on consensus. Rather, they would ultimately have to be substantiated by a complex philosophical analysis. Whilst that is outside the scope of this book, we think it worth pointing out that the identified core values are highly congruent with much recent writing in moral philosophy, which seeks to affirm the importance of human life, and of treating people as ends in themselves and not simply as means to an end.[7]

But to say that the three core values have always characterized social work practice is much more doubtful. Partly this is because, in daily practice, acknowledged good standards 'are neither easily achieved nor automatically sustained', as Davies (1985, p. 236) himself points out. But more importantly, even what has been considered good social work practice in its day has not always fully endorsed respect, care and hope for persons (for example, the work of the Charity Organization Society in the 19th century). In the field of SIRs, we would argue that the practice which has least embodied the core values has been that most squarely based upon the 'hierarchical examination' tradition considered in Chapter 2. A strong normative commitment to the core values is therefore the likeliest way to minimize what we would see as the undesirable features of that tradition.

Implications of adherence to the core values

If the above argument is correct, an SIR, and the preparatory work which has gone into it, must at all times show care, respect and hope for the individual subject of the report; and this must be a paramount consideration for the report writer.

To say this might seem to imply much too romanticized a view of social work practice. Quite apart from the problem of caring for and respecting certain difficult clients (which might be regarded as an obstacle to care, respect and hope, but one which could be overcome with empathy and good training), surely there are situations where it simply is not possible fully to care for or respect one individual because of the competing demands on the social worker of another individual and his needs? Indeed, are not social work agencies themselves often statutorily required to balance the different interests of various clients, and does not the burden of such requirements lie heavily upon the individual social worker at the 'coalface'?

These are pertinent observations which cannot be lightly dismissed. They certainly lead to the kind of situation such as child care proceedings, where care, respect and hope for the parents has to be balanced against care, respect and hope for the child, and a difficult decision taken which may, for example, greatly upset the parents and seem to them to deny any care or respect for them.

But the situation in SIRs is rather different. As has been argued in Chapter 2, following Streatfeild, in the court situation it is unambiguously the court's job, not the report writer's, to decide upon the final sentence. It is for the court, therefore, to judge the seriousness of the offence and the nature of the penalty required in the public interest (taking into account also the interests of potential future victims). *Only* the court has this role, and indeed it must be so because only the court has all the information, from all relevant sources, which is necessary to perform the sentencing task. Thus the probation officer or social worker is freed, by the structural situation of the courtroom, to concentrate her focus upon the offender and what will maximize his future potential. To say this is not to advocate taking a romantic or unrealistic view of the offender and his social situation – indeed, we would argue that there must be a more hard-headed appraisal of the defendant's offending, and the risk of further offences, than has often been the case in previous social inquiry practice. Rather, the task is, within a framework of care, respect and hope for the defendant, to think creatively about maximizing his human possibilities, bearing in mind the real social situation in which he finds himself.

Should report writers recommend custodial sentences?

With this as background, we may now turn to the very practical and difficult question, hinted at in Chapter 1, about recommendations for custodial sentences. It has been seen that judges and magistrates sometimes criticize report writers who do not recommend custody in what the court regards as a clear custodial case, describing their reports in phrases such as 'hopelessly unrealistic' or even 'rubbish' (see *The Guardian,* 22 May 1985). But in the light of the preceding analysis, the key question is whether a custodial recommendation can be justified from the kind of perspective we have advocated, that is, a social work report embracing care, respect and hope for the offender, which seeks to think creatively about maximizing his human possibilities.

There are, perhaps, five main justifications which have been put forward by those who have advocated the use of custodial recommendations. It will be best to deal with them one by one.

(a)   *That custody is in the best interests of the client* (assuming that the client does not request custody: see (e) below). This used to be quite a frequent justification for custodial recommendations when it was believed that, for example, borstal training could have a very beneficial effect upon young adult offenders. The Streatfeild Report included among the possible opinions which a probation officer could 'properly express' the following example:

> It is unlikely that probation would make any significant contribution to diverting the offender from crime; borstal training/detention in a detention centre may be a more hopeful alternative. (para. 345(e))

However, research results now provide no support for offering opinions of this kind (see Chapter 2); the only safe assumption for the report writer is that a custodial sentence is no more and no less likely to prevent recidivism than a non-custodial sentence.[8] It follows that this research evidence about recidivism offers no clear support for this first justification. Moreover, since for the time being we are only considering custody from the viewpoint of the client's best interests, it is important also to note that there may be some undesirable side-effects of imprisonment, such as its possible effect on the offender's intelligence, self-confidence or personality; its effect on his wife and children or significant others; possible job or earnings losses, and so on. The research evidence about such side-effects is by no means definitive, and the effects are apparently less severe than some commentators have assumed, but, nevertheless, it is reasonably clear that adverse side-effects can occur.[9] Since, of course, such effects always militate *against* custody when looked at from the point of view of the client's interest, this reinforces the case against custodial recommendations grounded on this first justification.

One possible exception to the view reached above that custodial recommendations are not in the interest of the client may be in certain situations, involving mentally disturbed offenders, where the defendant's behaviour suggests that in future he may act in a way likely to endanger himself; but even in such rare cases, the report writer's task (given her professional qualifications) is limited to pointing out this possibility and suggesting that more expert opinions are obtained. These very unusual cases aside, there is no strength in this first justification.

(b) *That custody is in the best interests of society.* This is a perfectly proper view for the courts to adopt: it is quite reasonable for courts to take into account considerations of general deterrence, public safety, the seriousness of the offence, and so on, and, having considered such matters, to judge that in certain cases a custodial sentence is necessary in all the circumstances. But as has been argued in Chapter 2, the probation officer or social worker's role is not the same as that of the judge or magistrate. And we have to say unambiguously that it is never the report writer's task to recommend custody because she considers this would be in the best interests of society.

This is not to say that the report writer wholly ignores the wider society and concentrates solely on the individual offender. As argued more fully in later chapters, the report writer must take into account the likelihood of future offending by the defendant, and assess this carefully when considering possible community disposals – though she does this always from the point of view of thinking creatively about maximizing the offender's human possibilities.

Three examples may help to clarify the above remarks. The first would be a case of such seriousness that a custodial sentence could be the only possible result, for example armed bank robbery. Here of course the probation officer, if asked to write a report, would not recommend a non-custodial disposal – but equally, it is still not her job positively to recommend custody, or even indirectly to do so by circumlocution. Rather her task as a social worker is to write a report containing relevant social information, and to offer personal support and assistance to the client in the full knowledge that a long custodial sentence is coming his way.[10]

A second illustrative case would be one of sexual abuse by a father on his ten-year-old daughter. Such offences often cause lasting and severe damage to the personal development and well-being of the victim, and this must be fully acknowledged in the report. Hence, steps may well have to be taken, at least for a time, to remove the father from the home. But it does not follow that custody is the only way of doing this, and from the point of view of the father's development this will not be in his best interests (see above). Hence the report writer may want to consider suggesting an alternative address in the community, with restrictions on visiting the family home. If the father refuses to consider abiding by such proposed restrictions, the report writer could nevertheless in good faith report her proposals to the court while indicating that the defendant felt unable to comply with the suggestions made. Again, custody would not be recommended.

The third example would be the rather rare kind of case where the report writer genuinely considers that no community disposals can properly be offered or suggested to the court. A report writer would not, in our view, be justified in taking such a stance because of certain technical operational difficulties in providing supervision, for example, where the defendant works long or unsocial hours, lives far away, or leads an itinerant lifestyle; nor just because a previous attempt at supervision has proved difficult. Rather, this would be the kind of case where, for example, the report writer thought that colleagues and project workers might actually be personally endangered by supervision. Again in such circumstances it would be the report writer's job to inform the court that in her view, as a professional social worker (with all that that implies by way of commitment to social work values), there was genuinely no possibility of successfully pursuing a community disposal. It would, however, in our view be necessary in each case for the report writer to justify, in sound professional terms, why a negative judgement on this point had been reached. Once again, the report would not positively recommend custody.

Thus in these three instances it is seen that custodial recommendations (direct or indirect) are to be avoided, but nevertheless the report writer has given proper consideration, as a social worker, to the wider society within which she, the offender and the court all operate.

(c)   *To be perceived as 'realistic'*. As indicated in Chapter 1, many probation officers and social workers clearly dislike the pressure of the need to be 'realistic' in their recommendations, but feel obliged to go along with realism because of their position within the court structure. To ignore the pressures, they feel, would betray some clients because the report writer's credibility would be diminished, and therefore, even in apparently promising cases, future recommendations would not be followed. This argument was endorsed by a judge with whom we corresponded in the course of preparing this book; the consequence was, he felt, that probation officers should recommend custody in some cases in order to make non-custodial recommendations more acceptable to the bench in other cases. As Walker and Beaumont (1981, p.23) put it:

> The overall content of the report stays close to the court's own probable definition of relevance. Occasionally a probation officer may even feel the need to recommend imprisonment in a difficult case, *in order to retain general credibility.* [emphasis added]

Seductive as this argument may seem, we must be quite clear about what it entails. And what it entails is that some defendants are deliberately consigned to custody by the probation officer as a sacrifice for the hoped-for successes in other cases. So stated, the argument plainly entails using certain persons as means to gain ends for other persons. As such, it clearly contradicts that important ethical tradition of always treating persons as ends, a tradition which, as has been seen, lies at the heart of our three social work core values.

(d) *'Tactical' recommendations for custody.* This argument for custodial recommendations is rather different from the previous one. It does not entail making custodial recommendations in one case in order to maximize non-custodial possibilities in another; rather it involves deliberately recommending a specific low-tariff custodial sentence because of the belief that the bench has in mind a higher-tariff custodial sentence. The most obvious example has been in the young offender field, where report writers have sometimes recommended a detention centre sentence, believing that youth custody is otherwise the probable outcome.

From the point of view of this book, with its stress on social work-based reports, this tactic has the obvious drawback that the report writer is prevented from offering to the court a set of non-custodial possibilities which can be justified in social work terms. Moreover, the tactic hinges upon the assumption that the officer is correct in her view that at least a short custodial sentence is the inevitable outcome. But research clearly shows that levels of agreement between bench and social worker on the likely sentence are not 100 per cent, and moreover that in certain instances the social worker, by recommending custody, can actually *increase* the likelihood of that disposal (Hine *et al.* 1978). It follows that the tactic, however laudable it might seem to the report writer, could actually achieve the opposite of what is intended. Hence, from the point of view of report writing committed to respect, care and hope for the defendant, this tactic is impossible to justify.

(e)   *Defendant prefers custody.* The final possible justification for custodial recommendations arises in those cases where the defendant actually requests custody during discussions with the report writer, and maintains this request throughout.

We think there are three main situations in which the defendant may make such a request. First, he may face difficult family or other social circumstances or responsibilities which he wishes to avoid by a 'cooling-off' period in prison (for example, major family conflicts or possible underworld 'comebacks'). Secondly, he may have many outstanding legal obligations arising from previous convictions (for example unpaid fines, unfinished community service hours) and may therefore prefer to 'clear the decks' by a custodial sentence embracing the current and previous offences. Thirdly, he may consider that a short custodial sentence would actually be preferable (by virtue of being a less severe or extended form of social control) to the non-custodial 'package' that is being suggested by the probation officer or social worker. For example, in juvenile cases the defendant may prefer a short detention centre sentence to a 'heavy-end' intensive intermediate treatment package involving perhaps four nights a week of intensive groupwork plus an element of 'tracking'.

In each of these cases, we think it is clear that the value of 'respect for persons' enjoins the report writer to inform the court that, after careful discussion with the report writer, the defendant's view is that he prefers custody – and to indicate to the court the reasons for the defendant's preference. However, the 'care' and 'hope' values may in this instance mean that the report writer will want to indicate that she cannot fully share the defendant's preference, and that there may be other ways of dealing with the issues raised by the defendant than by custody (such matters should, of course, have been fully discussed during the preparation of the report). This may be particularly the case in the first two categories we have mentioned above, and the alternatives may include family therapy, working through residual court obligations in liaison with the clerk's department, and so on. As regards the third type of case, we would suggest that if after discussion the defendant continues to consider the non-custodial package to be a more stringent alternative than custody, then the report writer should consider whether the defendant is right (leading to modification of the 'package') or, alternatively, should be prepared to justify it explicitly to the court in the light of the defendant's perception.

Thus, even in these cases, we think that the number of occasions when a report writer will want to recommend custody by endorsing the defendant's view will be very small indeed, if they exist at all.

The above five possible reasons for recommending custody have been of the 'direct' kind, that is, a positive recommendation for custody. It is also possible, however, for report writers to make 'indirect' recommendations for custody, or to imply that custody is the only available option, and Case C in Chapter 1 (see p.12) is an example of this practice. It should now be fairly clear that, in the light of the principles we have advocated, such practices are extremely difficult to justify, essentially for the same reasons that we have already considered in section (c) on 'realism' and section (d) on 'tactical' recommendations.

Thus we conclude that in almost every case the probation officer or social worker should not make a direct or indirect custodial recommendation.[11] For the sake of clarity, we should add that for this purpose 'custodial recommendation' includes recommendations for fully suspended sentences. The reason for this is that the relevant legislation and case-law makes clear that the suspended sentence is *a sentence of imprisonment which is held in suspense*, and that it should not be imposed on a defendant unless the court has considered and rejected all possible non-custodial options.[12] Moreover, research has shown that there is a strong 'kick-back' effect of suspended sentences – that is, defendants who breach suspended sentences are significantly more likely to receive a sentence of imprisonment on their next court appearance than are those receiving probation or community service, and the total length of the sentence of imprisonment may well be longer than would have been the case had an order other than suspended sentence been imposed in the first place (see Bottoms 1981).

The preceding argument seems to present a serious dilemma. We have argued that custodial recommendations cannot normally be justified, yet we have also seen that it is precisely such recommendations which are often regarded by courts and report writers as being necessary in some cases to maintain the overall credibility of the report writer (and her probation service or social work department) with the court. Together with other aspects of our analysis, this dilemma seems necessarily to raise the following major question, upon which the argument of much of the rest of the book must focus:

Can a form of SIR practice be developed which is faithful to the core values of social work, and truly uses social work knowledge and skills; which genuinely minimizes the 'hierarchical examination' element of the SIR; which eschews direct or indirect custodial recommendations; and yet which does not lose credibility with the courts on the grounds of lack of realism?

Briefly, our answer to this major question is 'yes'. The next three chapters are devoted to spelling out what such a form of SIR might look like.

Conclusion

It has been argued in this chapter that social inquiry practice must use social work knowledge and skills, and be conducted within the framework of social work values. In short, it has been said that the preparation of SIRs must be regarded as a social work task. We recognize that this is not a particularly fashionable stance to take[13], but it is a conclusion which seems to us to follow inexorably from a serious consideration of the question: by whom are SIRs written?

An insistence that report writing is a social work task is, we think, likely to prove a source both of weakness and of strength. It is a source of weakness because social work as an activity is very often misunderstood, misrepresented, and even derided by people in powerful positions in our society, especially in politics and the media. As Olive Stevenson (1974, quoted in Davies 1981, p.22) once put it:

> Society is deeply ambivalent about social work, asking it more and more to combat the alienation of a technological age, yet resenting its growing power and quick to point harshly to its failures, especially those in relation to functions of social control.

This general weakness of social work in relation to powerful wider audiences is certainly of importance in court-based social work, since judges and magistrates undoubtedly sometimes share these negative perceptions of social work as an activity. It is the task of those in senior managerial positions in the probation service and social services departments to try to counteract such images so far as possible (while frankly admitting genuine mistakes and failures by the agency). It is also their task, we think, to seek to show that explicitly social-work-based SIRs can be of value to sentencers, a point which should become clearer in the course of the next three chapters.

But there are also some very positive consequences of an emphasis upon SIR preparation as a social work task. Our experience suggests that, because of the many difficulties and dilemmas of SIR practice, it is all too easy for practitioners and managers to lose any clear vision of what SIRs are supposed to be and to achieve. To say unequivocally that social inquiry practice *is* a form of social work practice, and that SIRs *are* social work documents, can, in our experience, be a source of strength and of self-confidence to practitioners, enabling them to relate their SIR practice much more coherently to their professional social work training and experience. Of course, it is also essential for report writers to remember that SIRs are not general social work documents, and certainly not social histories, but are written for a specific audience (the court) for a specific purpose. But the combination of the 'for whom' and the 'by whom' questions posed at the beginning of this chapter produces the powerful answer: *Social inquiry reports are social work documents written for courts, to help them to determine what should happen to an offender as a consequence of the commission of a proved offence.*

The clear focus for social inquiry practice provided by this answer may also be of value to people other than probation officers and social workers. In particular, the explicit identification of SIRs as court-focused documents written using social work knowledge and skills, and embodying social work values, may help judges and magistrates to become clearer about what they can expect from SIRs, and more aware of some of the possibilities which are offered by them.

Notes

1   However, for reasons which should be clear from our discussion in Chapter 2, we consider that, in Giller's answer, the words 'to determine' should preferably read 'to help them to determine'. We use the latter form of words in the conclusion to this chapter.

2   It will be recalled (see Chapter 2) that Henri Giller does not consider SIRs to be social work documents. As argued in Chapter 2, however, Giller's understanding of this term seems to be limited to documents resembling social histories; he excludes many of these wider elements, especially social work values.

3   The elements of social work knowledge which we have identified in this passage are derived partly from Davies's work (Davies 1985, pp. 22-3), though we would place rather more importance than Davies does upon an understanding of basic social science.

4   In our view, the formulation 'respect for *persons*' has greater depth and humanness than 'respect for *individuals*', though we accept that this is a fine distinction.

5   There are, of course, difficulties about this concept in the case of some clients, notably the mentally handicapped, the mentally ill, and the senile. In the case of such clients, we would argue that 'respect for persons' should still be a core value so far as practicable, and that in any event the probation officer or social worker should always ask herself the question 'what would this client choose if he had his full faculties?'

6   This concept is also broad enough to embrace an aspiration which is increasingly being seen as important within social work, namely the aspiration that the client may himself use his personality and skills to help others in the community in the future.

7   See, for example, Dworkin (1977), Gewirth (1978) and Duff (1986). The means/end dictum derives from Immanuel Kant: 'act in such a way that you always treat humanity, whether in your own person or in the person of any other, never simply as a means, but always at the same time as an end' (see Paton 1948, p.91).

8   This is clearly the case for offenders who are before the courts on a second or subsequent conviction (that is, the great majority of those sent to prison). There is some tentative evidence that first offenders sent to prison might have slightly better than average reconviction rates, but for methodological reasons it is in our view unwise to rely on this finding. See generally the discussion in Walker (1985) Chapter 6, especially pp. 88-9.

9   Relevant issues are carefully discussed in Walker (1985, Chapter 11).

10   Home Office Circular 92/1986, para. 17, recommends that SIRs 'should not be prepared as a matter of routine ... in cases of serious and repeated offending where a custodial sentence is virtually inevitable'. This suggestion has, however, been argued against by many in the probation service because of the lack of predictability of the 'inevitability' of custody, and therefore the possible loss of opportunities for arguing in favour of community disposals: see Chapter 7 for a fuller discussion.

11   Willis (1986, p.34) argues against taking such a position, *inter alia* on the alleged ground that 'these fine sentiments contain a logical blunder. Non-custodial recommendations only make sense if they are set against the possibility of custodial ones, just as passing an examination is only credible when it is set against the possibility of failure. It is illegitimate artificially to discard one of two mutually exclusive alternatives (custodial or non-custodial recommendations) and pretend that what is left is a genuine choice'. The 'logical blunder', however, is Willis's. He makes no distinction between the role and functions of the *court*, and the role and function of the *report writer;* when this distinction is considered, his supposedly knock-down argument withers away.

12   See Powers of Criminal Courts Act 1973, s.22 (2); and R.v. O'Keefe (1968) 53 Cr. App. R. 91.

13   The role of report writer as social worker is not much emphasized, for example in the 1986 Home Office Circular or in the DHSS (1987) booklet on *Reports to Courts.*

4 Information relevant to offending

We saw in Chapter 2 that the Streatfeild Committee of 1961 identified three main elements of an SIR. It was also argued, that these three elements, somewhat reformulated, still formed a valuable framework for SIR practice. The three elements, as reformulated, are:

(a) information about the social background of the offender which is relevant to the court's assessment of his culpability;

(b) information about the social background and present situation of the offender which is relevant to some consideration of his future prospects;

(c) suggestions to the court concerning sentencing options, but not in a form indicating that the suggestions relate to all the considerations which the court has to address.

In this and the next two chapters, these three main elements of the SIR are considered. We begin with what the Streatfeild Committee called 'information relevant to culpability'.

The Streatfeild Report was not very specific about how 'information relevant to culpability' was to be presented in SIRs. It observed that 'individual cases vary widely', and that 'a report should not follow a stereotyped form'. It agreed, however, with the National Association of Probation Officers that in most cases relevant social information should include, among other things:

> essential details of the offender's home surroundings, and family background; his attitude to his family and their response to him; his school and work record and spare-time activities; his attitude to his employment; his attitude to the present offence; his attitude and response to previous treatment following any previous convictions; detailed histories about relevant physical and mental conditions; an assessment of personality and character. (para. 336)

As we noted in Chapter 2, the Streatfeild Committee went on to say that, at that time, information relevant to culpability and information relevant to future prospects were usually treated as one and the same; and it confessed that this much was implied by the generality of the list of factors it had given (see above). The committee looked forward to a time when a clearer distinction between the two kinds of information might be made. We believe that this can now be achieved, and that it is possible to identify and to use different frameworks for gathering and presenting information relevant to offending, and information relevant to future prospects.

One further observation about the Streatfeild Report should perhaps be made. Although the report spoke of 'information relevant to culpability', the types of information it expected would be supplied under this heading were mostly *not* about offences and offending as such, but about general social background (see the quotation above). A similar approach has been followed in traditional SIR practice, where reports have typically said little or nothing specifically about offences and offending behaviour; the three case examples in Chapter 1 are a good example of this. There are, no doubt, a number of reasons for this traditional practice, including perhaps (a) a general tendency in social work education and early professional experience to spend a lot of time on personal and family problems and little on offending as such; (b) a wish not to cause potential difficulty and embarrassment in a social worker-client relationship by dwelling too much upon the disagreeable; and (c) on some occasions at least, the adoption of a conscious tactical view that giving offending too high a profile within a court report might highlight it too much and thus perhaps increase the penalty for the offender (on this point see further below).

Interestingly, courts have sometimes seemed to endorse the absence of discussion of offending within SIRs. In the first place, they have objected to over-long reports, thus perhaps inhibiting inclusion of additional material about offences and offending. Secondly, magistrates and judges have sometimes said that an account of the circumstances of the offence simply duplicates the information already provided – as they see it – by the prosecution or the defence. Thirdly, in one piece of Scottish research some sheriffs (sentencers), while endorsing the inclusion of comments about the offender's attitude to the offence, said they objected to a discussion of the circumstances of the offence, mainly because 'it led to complications, especially when the facts of the offence had been the subject of dispute' (Curran and Chambers 1982, p.112).

In contrast to all this, as was seen in Chapter 1, Home Office Circular 92/1986, and the DHSS booklet on *Reports to Courts* (1987), both advise report writers to make offending behaviour a central feature of their reports; and other recent writers and practitioners have taken the same view. We strongly endorse this approach, since the reason that the defendant is before the court is because he has committed an offence, and it is strange if this fact is not centrally acknowledged and explored in the report.[1] For this and other reasons (see further below) we prefer the term 'information relevant to offending' as against Streatfeild's 'information relevant to culpability'.

But how is information of this sort to be presented? In Chapter 3, we argued for the view that the SIR is a social work document, in which the report writer uses social work knowledge and skills within a framework of social work values. Applying that perspective to the presentation of information about offending, we think that the social worker's task is: *to use social work knowledge and skills to set the offence, and any offending history, in the offender's social context.*

Our formulation is very close to (though it was developed before the publication of) the recent Home Office statement that 'the feature which distinguishes [the SIR] from other reports is that it should set the offending behaviour into the individual's social context, [and] examine the offender's view of that behaviour' (HOC 92/1986, para. 5). By satisfactorily accomplishing this task, we believe that report writers can help courts by presenting information about offending different from, but complementary to, what may already have been said by the prosecution and/or the defence lawyer.

What does the term 'social context' mean? We cannot speak for the Home Office, but for us this concept is most usefully understood as encompassing the three separate aspects of *structure, culture,* and *biography* (see Critcher 1976). As Peter Raynor (1980) explained these ideas in an article on SIRs:

> The constraints of 'structure' are those basic economic and material factors which set the limits of an individual's opportunities, and the constraints of 'culture' are the strengths and weaknesses of the way he has learned, along with other members of his social group, to assimilate, make sense of, and operate within the limits of structure. 'Biography' refers to the multitude of contingencies or accidents of experience that distinguish one individual from another, even within the same cultural and structural space.

Although Raynor's article is in our judgement one of the most stimulating and incisive pieces of writing on SIRs in recent years, it is noticeable that he seems to restrict the use of the structure/culture/biography framework to a discussion of the social information section of the SIR. When he turns to the current offence, he says:

> It is only by understanding, as far as possible, the offender's own view

of the offence and its circumstances that we can begin to think about what he intended, and how far he had a clear understanding of what was going on ... The task of acquiring it needs to be approached with what David Matza (1969) calls 'appreciation', that is, the attempt to understand the offender's perspective 'from the inside'.

While this is correct as far as it goes, in our view it does not go far enough. To 'appreciation' (a concept akin to the social work concept of empathy) should be added the structural and cultural contexts previously mentioned by Raynor. Hence, the social worker's job is to set offending in its social context for the court using these three concepts. The key question for the report writer to consider is, we would suggest: *why and how did this particular offender, with his particular social background (including offending history), get into this particular situation and then offend?*[2]

Clearly, the training and professional preoccupations of lawyers, whether they be acting for the prosecution or the defence, do not equip them to answer a question of this kind. By contrast, the social worker should be able to do so by virtue of her training and professional experience.

It is worth staying with the lawyer/social worker comparison a moment longer. It has sometimes been suggested (by magistrates, for example), that an SIR which discusses offences is just a disguised version of a defence plea in mitigation. The Scottish researchers Curran and Chambers (1982, p.82) took a not dissimilar view, arguing that the difference 'resides not in the information *per se* but in its presentation'. We would respectfully disagree. The fundamental purpose of a plea in mitigation is to *minimize guilt,* and sometimes even to try to *excuse*; by contrast, the task of the social worker writing about offending is, in our view, not to excuse or to minimize but to *explain*, in the terms outlined in the previous paragraph. The difference between excusing and explaining may seem to be a fine one; but we think it is of fundamental importance.

Case example D

What does all this mean in practice? To illustrate the possibilities, and to move the discussion on to a more practical plane, let us at this point introduce part of a recently written SIR for the Crown Court which attempted to take offending behaviour as its central focus. The case involved a 28-year-old man facing four charges of buggery, one of gross indecency and three of indecent assault on young males. The part of the report which looked backward to the offences and social history reads as follows:

Offences:

2 I understand Mr Jenkins will be pleading guilty to eight charges, arising out of sexual relationships over several years with several boys. The matters came to the attention of the police following an incident in February when Mr Jenkins is said to have indecently assaulted Tom Smith aged thirteen years. Tom Smith had been invited to stay at Mr Jenkins's house because of problems that the boy was experiencing at that time with his stepfather. Mr Jenkins has described the details of that evening (reading human biology books lying together on the floor, trying to help the boy undress for a bath, etc.) until Tom Smith ran off home at 1.00 a.m., obviously scared by Mr Jenkins's apparent advances. Mr Jenkins admitted indecent assault to the police when questioned, and subsequently revealed to them details about the other more serious matters before the court today.

3 Three charges of buggery and one of gross indecency relate to a sexual relationship that Mr Jenkins conducted intermittently for some twelve to eighteen months with Eddie Thomas, initially aged ten years when they met whilst Mr Jenkins was involved in running a Life Boys' camping trip. The lad later stopped at Mr Jenkins's house on several occasions, following family problems with his own father. Mr Jenkins recalls that Eddie Thomas was a willing partner, and that his original intention to comfort the lad led to sexual arousal for both.

4 One charge of buggery, and a charge of indecent assault, relate to a relationship that Mr Jenkins conducted with Nigel Valentine aged fifteen years at the time. Mr Jenkins tells me that the boy was also experiencing family problems, and was in the care of the local authority: he recalls that they grew attached to one another over a period of some months, sexual activity taking place when Nigel Valentine stayed at Mr Jenkins's house.

5 The defendant is also charged with indecent assault on Simon Yates, aged ten years. Most of the offences seem to have stemmed from Mr Jenkins's willingness to help young lads whom he saw as having family problems; he feels that despite the abuse of trust and responsibility inherent in the relationships, he never hurt a boy, and was never violent. I understand Mr Jenkins has no previous convictions.

Personal and family background:

6 From a working-class Baptist family, Mr Jenkins is the second youngest of nine children, born and brought up in the mining village of Cwm, Gwent. When he was nine years old, he recalls his father died in a bizarre fashion, falling into the fire at home, apparently having blacked out. Mr Jenkins feels that he was particularly affected, having a close relationship as the youngest son, and that ever since he has felt abandoned and isolated even within his own family. The family were poverty stricken, and Mr Jenkins recounts that he came to worry more and more, identifying very much with his hardworking mother. Within the home, however, Mr Jenkins seems to have been the victim of bullying, especially by the eldest son of the family, against whose domestic tyranny he particularly rebelled.

7 Mr Jenkins completed secondary education, and subsequently worked for an engineering firm, as a labourer, and in painting and decorating; since 1979 however he has been employed as a face worker at the local colliery. Following his arrest in August last year he was eventually obliged to live away from his home: his job is still said to be open to him, but he is uncertain as to whether he could ever face his colleagues again.

8 Mr Jenkins married in 1981; the relationship seems to have been particularly unrewarding for both partners; he recounts that they rarely communicated, and that his wife spent most of her time with her mother, being rarely in the home. Their sex life was non-existent, and they in fact separated when news of his offence surfaced.

9 Throughout his adult life Mr Jenkins has been directly involved in the care of his increasingly dependent mother. Having lived with her until his marriage, her arthritic condition worsened, necessitating a move to a nearby old people's flat, so that Mr Jenkins could carry on caring for her. Mr Jenkins feels angry and guilty as regards his mother: angry at the way the rest of his brothers and sisters had left the burden of her care to him, and guilty that he has let her down, and that he has caused her so much shame.

10 The demands of looking after his mother have left Mr Jenkins with little time for leisure, although he does have some hobbies, and was a regular church attender. What spare time he does have he devoted to youth work, in particular the Boys Brigade and Life Boys. He first became involved some ten years ago: his interest was sustained by the friendship of the B.B. leader, an older man who treated Mr Jenkins with respect, as an equal, unlike his family or most other people he knew. When this person died unexpectedly some two years ago, Mr Jenkins recalls that he again felt the same degree of loss and isolation that he remembered from his father's death.

Current circumstances:

11 Since his release from custodial remand seven months ago, Mr Jenkins has been in receipt of benefits and living in a lodging house at the address overleaf. He manages his limited finances adequately, and has begun to make some friends.

12 Following his collapse when arrested, Mr Jenkins seems to have undergone experiences akin to a mental breakdown. Some weeks later he attempted suicide, and has since been attending a local psychiatric day centre, initially full-time, now for one day per week. He values the routine, and the social contacts it provides. Mr Jenkins recalls that he had a similar breakdown when he was eleven or twelve, said at the time to be a delayed response to his father's death.

Discussion:

13 The root causes of this defendant's offending behaviour lie in the sense of isolation he felt in his family, and latterly in the community. Although Mr Jenkins does not identify himself as homosexual, he admits that he has not had satisfying sexual relationships with women, and recounts that from the age of ten years, to about fourteen years, he was himself the

victim of sexual abuse at the hands of two neighbouring boys, several years his senior. He remembers that this early sexual activity, at a time when he was emotionally vulnerable and still in mourning, provided him with comfort and companionship.

14 Over the last three or four months Mr Jenkins has been able to reflect at length on his offending, and is able to acknowledge that, as a person who needed to feel loved, and to give love, he derived a degree of comfort from sexual relations he initiated with the boys. He felt particularly close to Nigel Valentine and Eddie Thomas as companions, although for most of the boys their undemanding attentions also made him feel important and worthwhile.

15 His feeling that his victims got something in return from the relationships served to outweigh his reservations: he often felt scared and nervous, and was forever frightened of the consequences of discovery. He initially enjoyed the sexual activity, but found that it filled him with self-loathing, and that he continued it partly as a way of expressing companionship, and partly for fear of upsetting the boys and thus precipitating his discovery. He increasingly came to feel that the sexual side of the relationship was nullifying all the good he felt he was doing (by befriending the boys with problems similar to the ones he had experienced in his childhood), and with hindsight he is now sincerely relieved that these matters finally came out into the open. He has come to realize that his actions were wrong and misguided: he considers that his arrest has served to highlight just what a mess his emotional life was in. Indeed he feels that he himself was more in need of help and care than those to whom he offered help.

16 Mr Jenkins describes the last three or four years as like 'living in a nightmare'. He has found the results of his public humiliation have both confirmed his fears (he has lost his job, his marriage, his home and a lot of friends, as well as being exiled from his community) and provided him with a sense of having come through an ordeal. He is relieved that his family has responded better than he expected, and whilst saddened by the shock he has caused his mother, he is also relieved that others in the family have taken on the burden of her care that the removal from his home town meant he could no longer meet.

This report is very long – perhaps over-long – and the argument could be more tightly structured. Despite these criticisms, a number of positive features of the report are worth noticing. First, the discussion of the offences seems to us to be clearly conducted with a strong sense of 'appreciation' or empathy, but also not losing sight of cultural and biographical factors (because of the nature of the offence social-structural factors are perhaps less prominent than they would be for most offenders). Secondly, while some of the details of the social history are superfluous, for the most part the social history has been used to explain the defendant's offending. Thus social work knowledge and skills have clearly been put to use, and the whole is also permeated by social work values, conveying, as Raynor (1980, p.82) put it in another context, 'a respect for the value of persons despite their behaviour, but without overlooking the behaviour'. Finally, we would suggest that it is the very specificity of factual information concerning the offences at the beginning of the report (paras 1-5) which has allowed the probation officer to make her subsequent assessment (in paras 13-15) with such clarity and understanding.

Further issues
So far in this chapter we have outlined some key ideas underpinning the discussion of offending in SIRs, and we have then illustrated some of these ideas by means of a case example. We now need to develop a number of issues and implications which arise from what has been said.

Social history
Many if not most SIRs have traditionally contained a section which sets out the offender's social history. But, as noted in Chapter 2, Streatfeild's threefold scheme about SIR content, which we are following (with modifications) in Chapters 4-6, does *not* contain any such specific section. Rather, the implication is that personal/social/ developmental history will be used in the report, but *only* to illuminate offending (see this Chapter), future prospects (Chapter 5) or options as to disposal (Chapter 6).

This point, if taken seriously, has a number of detailed implications. One obviously affects the traditional layout and content of reports. Another is that some of the information included in the traditional SIR will be excluded (where it does not relate directly to offending, future prospects, or options); while sometimes with this new focus the report writer may include information in a specific case which she otherwise would not have done, or include it within a more disciplined and purposeful framework. 'Free-floating' social information, as such, should not appear.

The report writer's role
Streatfeild spoke of: information about the social and domestic background of the offender which is relevant to *the court's assessment* of his culpability. (para. 335 (a)) [emphasis added].

By implication, the Streatfeild Committee was clearly indicating that the court makes the culpability assessment, while the report writer provides information upon which such an assessment can be based.

This view contains both an important truth and an oversimplification. The important truth is that, at the end of the day, it is the court which has to judge the offending; the report is ancillary to that process. The oversimplification lies in the suggestion that 'information' or 'facts' are independently available to present to the court, uncontaminated by theoretical frameworks or the values of those who collect them, which is not the case. Nevertheless, what the report writer puts in her report should not be a collection of her personal prejudices (even though some personal values will inevitably colour the contents). There is information out there to be collected, and it is the report writer's job to collect it (using her social work knowledge and skills), and then to present it to the court through the *professional* value-system which was outlined in Chapter 3.

The report thus constituted is then presented to the court, which judges the offending having taken into account all the information presented to it from diverse sources, and bearing in mind its own responsibility for the public good as well as the offender's good.

Peter Raynor (1980) summarizes all this well when he says:

> Nor am I advocating that probation officers themselves take on the task of moral evaluation in sentencing – simply that they recognize that this is an important use of the information they provide in the sentencing process ... The report does not determine the moral evaluation, but contains some of the [information and discussion] on which the sentencer can base a moral evaluation.[3]

Culpability

Talk of 'moral evaluation' in a sentencing context clearly links with the concept of 'culpability', which as we have seen was a central concept in the Streatfeild Committee's analysis.

We have consciously chosen to move away from Streatfeild's terminology of 'information relevant to the assessment of culpability' and to substitute 'information relevant to offending'. This choice has been made for three reasons. First, it helps to emphasize that offending behaviour should be directly discussed in the report (see above). Secondly, 'culpability', at least in normal usage, is restricted to an assessment of the current offence rather than the offending history as a whole (the lack of previous offending may reduce culpability, but past offences cannot increase the culpability of the present offence: Emmins 1984, pp. 272-4); by contrast, we think it is the report writer's task to set both the current offence and previous offending in its social context. Thirdly, the concept 'culpability', while well understood by lawyers in a sentencing context, carries for many lay-people (including magistrates) and for social workers a rather heavy moral tone which goes well beyond the technical understanding and usage of the term in legal circles.

Despite this, no serious student of sentencing, and of the role of SIRs in the sentencing process, can avoid considering culpability. Raynor (1980) again puts the point well. Legal guilt is established by a conviction, but the court needs to go on to consider the degree of blameworthiness of the offender, which

> may depend, for instance, on what I intended to do; on whether I was adequately informed about the circumstances in which I acted; on whether I was capable of alternative courses of action; on whether I was under unusual stress; on whether I was confused; or on whether I was brought up in such a way as not to regard my action as wrong. Many possible circumstances could allow my action to be seen as less than wholly blameworthy, or less than deliberately criminal.

In order to assess some of these matters properly, the court has to rely, amongst other things, upon the information provided in the SIR. These matters will include information about the offender's reported motivation and his attitude to the offence, which in turn must be based on careful discussion with the offender. But this is not to say that the report writer necessarily reports the offender's expressed motivation and attitude. It is proper, if the report writer holds a view, for her to state that view, provided that this is done in a way which is consistent with the values outlined in Chapter 3, which means *inter alia* that any disagreement with the offender's own assessment must have been fully explained to and discussed with him. An example of this would be where an offender appeared to the report writer to be either minimizing or overstressing his responsibility in the commission of the offence.

We have indicated what discussing matters relevant to culpability involves; it is just as important to see what it does not mean. Not infrequently in SIR writing one may come across covert character assessments which are in effect designed to influence the court's view of the offender's degree of culpability; an example would be a phrase such as 'he presents as a surly and truculent young man'. Phrases of this sort are often clearly connected with the relationship between report writer and client at the SIR interview (or in previous relationships), and they often seem not to have been carefully discussed with the offender. Nor do they necessarily have anything at all to do with a proper assessment of the offender's attitude to and motivation for offending, even though they may be read that way by the court. As such, this kind of 'smuggling-in' of value-statements masquerading as having to do with assessing culpability are clearly not congruent with the social work values outlined in Chapter 3.

A word on victims
We have advocated offence-specific discussion in SIRs, and most offences have a victim. Particularly in the light of the recent rise of the victims movement in various countries (the growth of victim compensation, victims' support schemes, etc.) it might fairly be asked whether we are therefore arguing that matters such as the extent of injury or loss to the victim, his/her emotional stress in reaction to the offence, his/her attitude to the offender, etc. should be included in the SIR. Such a question is particularly pertinent given that some states in the USA now require some information of this kind in pre-sentence reports (see Harding 1982, p.43).

The English SIR has traditionally been rather different from the American pre-sentence report, not least because English probation officers, unlike their American counterparts, see their role as being predominantly social workers with offenders rather than correctional agents. Within this tradition, with its empathy for the offender, careful reporting on the victim's attitude, loss, etc. would not be easy to achieve if undertaken by the same officer in the same report.[4] It may be that in the future the probation service may be required to report on such matters, but if so this would be best done in a separate report in which the social work values of respect for persons etc. would be applied from the victim's perspective. In the meantime, we would suggest that report writers do not stray too far into the realms of victimology in their present social inquiry practice, though that is not to say that they should in any way minimize the seriousness of the harm which an offender may have caused to the victim.[5]

Offending history
In the first few pages of this chapter we indicated our general approach to writing about offending in SIRs, in a way which included previous offences as well as the current offence. Subsequently, we have concentrated on the current offence, for example in case

example D where there were no previous convictions.

The current offence is usually rightly the main focus of the report writer's attention, because it is for that offence that the offender is to be sentenced. But this does not mean that previous offending is irrelevant, and it should always be carefully discussed with the defendant even if little is ultimately said in the SIR. The key test for inclusion in the report has to be current relevance; an offence of a very similar kind committed recently is clearly more worthy of discussion than a dissimilar offence committed several years ago. Equally, special attention might be focused upon a previous offence for which a suspended sentence or community disposal was ordered, for the breach of which the offender is currently before the court in addition to his main offence. Other matters of current relevance might include, for example, a considerable gap in offending immediately before the present court appearance despite a long previous criminal history.

It will be clear from the above that the not infrequent practice of simply alluding to previous offending in a report by saying 'the court will be aware of the defendant's antecedents' is not adequate, since it does not reflect any informed appraisal from a social work perspective. At the very least, a report writer who chooses to say little about previous offending should indicate the reasons for this in the report: for example, 'the only previous offence is of a very different nature and is not relevant to an understanding of this offence'.

Detrimental to offenders

Could it be the case that a concentration upon the discussion of offending in SIRs, perhaps particularly when conducted at the level of detail exemplified in case example D, might be detrimental to the offender's immediate interests? This is a very important issue which has not been sufficiently discussed as official policy has moved towards a greater concentration on offences in SIR writing (see Chapter 1). In considering this question, we think there are three main types of situation where a detrimental effect might be said to occur, and these need to be discussed separately.

The first type of situation is where alleged offences which have not been charged come to the notice of the report writer from sources other than the offender.[6] This is quite likely to occur in situations where a probation or social work team is engaged extensively in community or neighbourhood work, with many informal contacts between professional workers and members of the public in detached settings: in such situations, it is not unusual for people in the community to talk about others, including their undetected offending, to the agency worker. Suppose then that a local youth is brought before the court on a single charge of taking a car, and that casual informal mention is made to the expected report writer that this is in fact a fairly regular pattern of activity which has been going on for some months. Our view of this situation would be: (i) that any social work agency working in this detached way must have some general rules as to how to handle this kind of information, whether or not occurring in the context of an impending court appearance (for example, perhaps through a steering committee for the project – see Hugman 1977), but it would be straying too far from our subject to discuss the details of this; (ii) that nevertheless the report writer should *not* include this material in her SIR because it has no proper evidential status in a court context; but that (iii) the report writer can and should discuss the matter with the offender and, if he agrees, contact the defence solicitor with a suggestion that, if agreed with the client, additional offences could be taken into consideration at the court appearance (if so, the report could be modified appropriately). This approach would ensure that the report was not detrimental to the offender's interest.

The second type of situation to be considered is where extraneous social information possibly detrimental to the offender, but which may contribute to an understanding of the offence, comes to the report writer's notice during SIR interviews. An example of this occurred a few years ago in a report being prepared by one of the authors: a youth already on probation named Ernie Robinson was facing a series of charges for property offences, including the taking of a car, and, with others, setting fire to it and pushing it into a lake. During a home visit, Ernie's mother revealed to the probation officer that Ernie's behaviour had been very unstable in the last month, and that he had, among other things, thrown a vegetable knife across the kitchen at his mother, and kicked his pregnant girlfriend in the stomach. The dilemma for the officer was whether to introduce such information into the SIR, and if so how. Since the officer believed that these incidents were certainly relevant to an understanding of Ernie's emotional state at the time of the offences charged, he did introduce the material (after discussing it with Ernie), but in the context of a request for a psychiatric report. We believe that this decision was justified, and would be so in similar situations, provided that: (i) the material really is relevant to an understanding of the present offence; and (ii) is used in a sensitive way consistent with the social work values explained in Chapter 3. This would be so even in cases where, unlike the Ernie example, the information revealed by, say, a spouse and other relatives was such as to make the offender appear to be chronically selfish and self-indulgent. In such a situation it would be more than ever important for the report writer to introduce the material, if relevant to the offence, only in a way which showed real empathy with the defendant's situation and which refused to join in any 'character-assassination' through the formal medium of the report. So handled, we doubt whether courts would treat the information as detrimental, as indeed the court did not in Ernie's case.

The third type of situation is one where the report writer includes considerable detail about the charged offence(s) and this might be thought detrimental to the offender's immediate interests. (Case example D might be thought to exemplify this). Here we need to be especially clear about what information the court is likely to receive from other sources. If, as will often happen, the prosecution introduces a detailed account of the offence, and what the SIR says is congruent with and does not in its details go beyond the prosecution's account, then there is no difficulty: the officer is simply placing that detail within a social work context and understanding. The potential difficulty arises where the defendant reveals to the report writer some details about a charged offence which are not in the prosecution's version of events: for example, that an attempted entry into a video shop to take goods was pre-planned rather than undertaken on the spur of the moment.

We think that in practice this problem will occur only very infrequently; nevertheless, it does present a very real dilemma. On the one hand, since it is the report writer's task to explain the offence in its social context to the court, it appears on the face of it proper to include this detail; and it should be remembered that if the report is being written in a way consistent with social work values and skills, the details will be presented in an empathetic way. On the other hand, it has to be recognized that the inclusion of additional details of this kind could lead to a more detrimental disposal, from the offender's point of view, than he would otherwise have received; and the offender may subsequently perceive this fact, causing lasting damage to the relationship between report writer and client.

There are no easy solutions to this dilemma, rare though it is, and the issue is probably only resolvable on a case-by-case basis and depending on the particular circumstances. But the dilemma does raise some important practice implications, especially as regards obtaining the prosecution's version of the offence(s), and explaining the social inquiry process to the defendant in a thorough and comprehensible manner: these issues are dealt with in the final section of this chapter.

Disputed facts
Earlier in this chapter, we noted that in some Scottish research, sheriffs disliked discussion of the circumstances of offences in SIRs because of legal complications, 'especially when the facts had been the subject of dispute' (Curran and Chambers 1982). This raises an important issue about what the report writer should do, in the approach which has been advocated in this chapter, if there are disputed facts relating to the offence, but the offender is nevertheless pleading guilty.

We are clear that the report writer should not attempt to comment on, or arbitrate in such a dispute – that is a matter for prosecution and defence counsel, and for the bench. However, this does not necessarily preclude any discussion of the offence in the SIR. For example, where two boys steal goods but dispute the value placed on the goods by the prosecution, that dispute can be noted in the report, but this would not impede a social-work-based discussion of the offence. This may also be the case in more serious offences, for example in a robbery charge where the defendant admits taking money from the victim by force, and admits carrying a knife, but denies that he used the knife in the course of the robbery.

However, if the disputed fact is very central to the offence admitted, it may be that the report writer is unable to comment constructively on the offence at all. In those circumstances, the report writer should seriously consider not preparing a report, despite the guilty plea, since the situation is in many ways analogous to a plea of not guilty.[8]

Practice matters
Before concluding this chapter, it is important that a few matters of practical detail which flow from the preceding discussion should be mentioned.

Thorough explanation of process
The social work value of 'respect for persons' requires that the report writer should, at the outset, explain to the defendant thoroughly and carefully everything that is involved in the process of preparing an SIR. It is inconsistent with that value to expect anyone (whether a

first or a recidivist offender) to be prepared to divulge very personal accounts of themselves and their offences without their knowing in advance what the stages and the end-product of the process are likely to be.

We think this explanation of process should be carried out at three different points in the inquiry. First, by the court duty officer who takes remand and referral details when the magistrates request a report or commit the defendant to the Crown Court; secondly, in the letter that the report writer sends out to the defendant suggesting an initial meeting (some probation services now send out a specifically-written information leaflet about the social inquiry process with this letter); and thirdly, at the start of that initial meeting. While this may sound over-elaborate, our experience suggests that explanations of process are too easily dispensed with, and building them in at different points seems to us to be a necessary safeguard for the defendant.

Obtaining the prosecution version of the offence and the police antecedents

In our experience, rarely does the report writer seek to obtain the prosecution's version of the offence, though in many areas (at least at Crown Court level) antecedent information about previous convictions is routinely supplied by the police. In our view it is vital that both these documents are obtained before the first SIR interview. If this is not done, and if the report writer nevertheless includes some discussion of the offence and offending history, she may run the risk of incurring the court's legitimate criticism for simply presenting the defendant's view without having discussed conflicting accounts with him. Additionally, she may risk including some details of the offence which are not in the prosecution's account, without knowing that she is doing so (see the discussion above). More positively, only if one knows the police version of the current offence, and the official record of previous convictions, can one properly discuss, explore and finally understand these incidents from the defendant's perspective.

It should be emphasized, however, that obtaining these documents does *not* mean that the report writer should necessarily include the information in them in her report. The primary purpose of obtaining the information is to improve the SIR interviews, not to duplicate written information for the court.

Interviewing implications
It should by now be clear that one important practical implication of this chapter is the need to obtain a clear and thorough view, in the interviews, of the defendant's perspective on his offending. In our experience, it is good practice always to start the interview with a discussion of the current offence and offending history, since this helps to marshal and keep relevant the subsequent obtaining of social information. Similarly, it is usually helpful to begin the report itself with a discussion of offending.

Social networks
SIRs have often included some discussion of family structure and relationships, employment history and perhaps organized leisure pursuits; but they more rarely include any account of wider social networks. Case A in Chapter 1 is a good example of this. That case also shows how what looks relevant to an explanation of the current offence – an approach made to Mr Bishop with regard to stolen goods – is referred to only very allusively (para. 7), though it may have taken place in what to the offender was an important or regular social context. This emphasizes that offending often takes place away from home, family, or employment, and so, if the focus is only on these matters and neglects wider networks, incomplete pictures of offending will emerge. In the terms used earlier in this chapter, this suggests that probation officers and social workers need to pay more attention to features of structure and of culture in their local areas if they are to improve their SIR preparation and writing. This is consistent with the message of Home Office Circular 92/1986 (see Chapter 1).

Conclusion
We have argued in this chapter for an approach to SIR writing which takes offences and offending behaviour much more seriously than has traditionally been the case in local practice (see the case examples in Chapter 1). We also believe that a sound examination of offending is an essential prerequisite for a proper consideration of future prospects – as we hope will become clear in the next chapter.

Notes
1   We are assuming here that SIRs will only be prepared on those who are pleading or have been found guilty: see further, Chapter 7.
2   Tutt (in Tutt and Giller 1984) has a not dissimilar formulation 'the social inquiry report needs to explain why this particular offence has occurred at this particular time and in this particular situation'.
3   In this quotation, we have substituted 'information and discussion' for Raynor's

original wording of 'facts'.

4   There is some empirical evidence which supports this view in Anne Celnick's (1984) evaluation of the probation-based Heeley Project in South Yorkshire (see pp. 253-6 and 271-3 of the report).

5   Readers who are sceptical of the dangers of straying into victimology should consider the article by Bartholomew and Lord (1975) in which, in our view, matters are taken to unjustifiable extremes.   In particular, the pre-sentence report in a rape case, reproduced and endorsed by the authors, fails to show any degree of respect or concern for the victim of the offence.

6   If the offender himself is the source of such information, we would suggest that the report writer should encourage him to tell the defence solicitor and the police about this (with a view to having the offence taken into consideration), and offer him every support in this course of action.   If the offender were unwilling to do this, we would recommend that the defence solicitor should nevertheless be told about the matter, so that he or she could form a judgement about how to proceed.

7   We would wish to emphasize that the report writer should not be going around the neighbourhood purposely eliciting information of this sort (in the manner of the inquiry agent described by Donzelot (1980): see Chapter 2). The information will have come to light, we are assuming, because of the relaxed and informal nature of the report writer's community involvement and community links.

8   In such circumstances, courts sometimes hold a special hearing to determine the facts (known as a 'Newton hearing' after the guidance given in R.v. Newton (1982) 77 Cr. App. R. 13): see Emmins (1985, pp.58-60).

5 Information relevant to future prospects

As indicated in Chapter 2, the sections of the SIR which deal with information about the offender's background and current situation can be best divided into a backward-looking consideration of offending and a forward-looking consideration of the offender's prospects.

Why and how should the forward-looking part of this task be accomplished? Two influential answers to this question have been the traditional 'treatment' approach, and the more recently formulated 'justice model'. The Streatfeild Report followed the former approach, and said that a probation officer could 'helpfully and properly' furnish the court with:

> Information about the offender and his surroundings which is relevant to the court's consideration of how his criminal career might be checked. (para. 335 (b))

One difficulty about this approach is, as seen in Chapter 2, that the disappointing results of treatment research conducted since Streatfeild's day have meant that there is no specific body of information available to sentencers or report writers as to how best to check a criminal career. More generally, also, Streatfeild's view was part of a 'scientistic' approach which is now hard to justify in the light of subsequent theoretical critiques (see Chapter 2, p.21).

A common reaction to the 'decline of treatment' has been the adoption of a 'justice model' approach to sentencing, not dissimilar to that of 18th century classical writers (see especially von Hirsch 1986). Justice model approaches of one kind or another have also found their way into social work discourse, especially in the juvenile field (see Morris and Giller 1987, Chapter 8). The justice model protests against what it sees as the excessive power often taken over individuals' lives in the name of 'treatment' or 'welfare', and prefers an approach in which the amount of punishment awarded by the court is determined primarily by the seriousness of the offending[1]; in its purest form, the model eschews completely any consideration, by either sentencer or report writer, of the offender's future behaviour and situation, including prospects of personal and social change as well as the risk of future re-offending.

There have been a number of general criticisms of the justice approach to sentencing, but we do not propose to discuss such matters here.[2] In this book, our principal concern throughout is with SIR writing from the point of view of the report writer, conceived as a social work task. From this perspective, there is a serious objection to abandoning any consideration of future prospects in the SIR; namely, that this would fail to communicate to sentencers any issues connected with what we have argued is a core social work value of 'hope for the future and recognition of clients' potential for survival and growth'. As argued below, however, acceptance of this point does not entail the inclusion in the report of a mass of personal information unrelated to offending; nor does it entail any view that sentencers should be encouraged to award greater or more intrusive penalties in the name of the offender's welfare (see Chapter 6).

Raynor (1980) has argued the case for a social work approach to SIR writing which both explores culpability (see Chapter 4) and looks forward to future possibilities. However, he identifies 'social information' mainly with a backward-looking approach; and the forward-looking part of the report he sees as being largely confined to the exploration, by the report writer and the offender, of a possible contractual basis upon which to offer to the court some suggestions for sentencing. While we would agree with much of Raynor's approach, we think it is important to identify an intermediate stage between the exploration of offending (see Chapter 4) and suggesting options to the court (see Chapter 6). This intermediate stage is part of the 'social information' in the report, but it is forward-looking: it considers the offender's future prospects from a social work perspective.

While for analytic purposes we have separated out this 'intermediate stage' of looking at future prospects, we want to stress that of course there is an intimate interlinking between the issues of considering offending, exploring future prospects, and suggesting options to the court. We have separated out the three topics for conceptual clarity, and to aid the thinking of practitioners, *not* because they are unconnected.

Risk, need and resources
How should an examination of the offender's future prospects be undertaken in practice?

Our answer to this question builds on the work of Curnock and Hardiker (1979), though it is not identical to it.[3] From a careful study of SIRs, some interviewing of probation officers about their reports, and the theoretical influence of Haines (1975), Curnock and Hardiker claimed that report writers often have implicitly in mind, in writing their reports, a balancing of the positive and negative features of the case under the threefold scheme of *risk, need,* and *resources.* When these three general concepts were introduced in the RSDO courses (see Preface) practitioners attending the courses found them a very helpful framework within which to think about offenders' future prospects. This threefold framework has been retained as the basis for this chapter, but Curnock and Hardiker's discussion of the three concepts has been considerably elaborated.

Risk

Although helpfully introducing the concept of 'risk', Curnock and Hardiker do little to specify what is meant by this idea in the context of SIR writing.[4]

We think it is important to distinguish between three kinds of risk, only the first two of which are the concern of the report writer. The first type is the risk of the offender re-offending; the second type is the risk of damage to the offender and his family and friends consequential on offending or likely offending; and the third type is the potential risk to possible future victims of the offender should he re-offend.

The third type of risk might seem at first sight to be very similar to the first. The difference is that the third type concentrates its attention upon the future potential victim as a person, the kind of loss or injury he or she might sustain, etc., whereas the first type of risk simply considers whether the offender is or is not likely to re-offend. Consideration of the third type is a matter exclusively for the court, as part of its role in the safeguarding of societal interests (see Chapters 2 and 3). But even when one is considering writing a report concentrating the focus upon the offender and what will maximize his future potential (see Chapter 3), it is vital to assess the risk of re-offending. Only if this is done does the report writer stand any chance of preparing a plan of action which may help the offender to avoid future trouble (see Chapter 6).

We will deal separately with the two kinds of risk which are of concern to the report writer, that is, the first and second kinds listed above.

Risk of re-offending

There are really two different sets of factors which may help the report writer to assess the likelihood of re-offending by the offender. These we may call (following Brearley 1982) predisposing hazards and situational hazards. 'Predisposing hazards' refer to existing features of a case which produce a particular likelihood or otherwise of re-offending; 'situational hazards' refer to situations in which the offender might find himself (or indeed engineer) and which are likely to increase or diminish the risk of offending.

When assessing *predisposing hazards,* report writers could usefully bear in mind a number of well-established findings from criminological research. These include the following:[5]

1   Number of previous convictions: the larger the number, the more likely it is that there will be a further conviction.
2   Current age: the younger the offender, the more likely he is to be reconvicted.
3   Gender: males are more likely to be reconvicted than females.[6]
4   Age at first conviction: the younger the age, the more likely the offender is to be reconvicted.
5   Length of time between last conviction and present offence: the shorter the gap, the more likely the offender is to re-offend.
6   Previous experience of institutions: the greater the experience, the more likely the offender is to re-offend.
7   Number of associates in current offence: the larger the number, the *less* likely it is that the offender will be reconvicted.[7]

In addition to these general findings which apply to all kinds of offenders, it is worth noting that there seem to be some predisposing features specific to particular crimes, for example a high rate of re-offending for burglary and robbery, and a low rate of re-offending for arson.[8]

These findings, of course, derive from complex pieces of statistical research. We are not suggesting that probation officers and social workers should attempt to obtain and use statistical data relating to these variables, but we do think that a general awareness of them is valuable to the report writer both in discussing future possibilities with the offender and in considering what material should form part of the final report.

Turning now to *situational hazards,* we have previously defined these as 'situations in which the offender might find himself (or engineer) and which are likely to increase or diminish the risk of offending'. What exactly does this mean?

The essential point is one familiar to all social workers, namely people's behaviour often varies when they are in different social situations. In the field of offending behaviour, well-known examples are first, the ex-adolescent tearaway who settles down and stops committing offences after forming a stable emotional relationship; and secondly, the rootless adult petty offender who is regularly reconvicted except at times when he is able to find a stable and caring place to live, such as a well-run hostel. Examples of situational hazards would include heavy drinking (a particular offender seems more likely to offend when he resorts to drink), employment situation, financial situation, aspects of leisure patterns, gambling, drug abuse, and so on. Whereas predisposing hazards are identified by research workers from large statistical samples, the identification of situational hazards depends upon a very close examination of the previous offending behaviour of the individual offender and the social situations in which it occurred, coupled with an analysis of the likely recurrence of such situations in his case. Thus, identifying likely situational hazards in a real sense requires social work skills and knowledge.

To illustrate the above discussion, let us consider a case example. Stuart, a married man aged 25, appeared before the Crown Court charged with (i) theft of lead piping from a derelict house, value £20; and (ii) theft of social security giro and attempting to cash same. At the time of the offences, he was the subject of a suspended sentence supervision order, previously imposed in the Crown Court, for an offence of burglary of a garage and theft of tyres (a pre-planned group burglary in which the garage safe had been the main target). He had five previous convictions, including the burglary; all of the others were for minor property offences. Previous orders given to Stuart included fines, probation and a community service order; he had, however, never been in prison save for seven days for non-payment of fine.

Stuart's version of the current offences was, first, that he was until recently living in a street of terraced houses due for demolition, so he took the opportunity to go into one of the vacated houses with his hacksaw and cut out the lead fittings (he was, he says, seen and 'shopped' by a 'nosey twat' of a neighbour); and, secondly, that Stuart's brother brought round a social security giro addressed to someone living in the same house as the brother, knowing that Stuart was 'often skint'. Stuart took the giro and tried to cash it at the post office, but the false identity was noticed. Stuart claimed that these offences, like most of his other crimes, occurred when he was particularly short of money. At such times, he said, he usually tried to borrow first, but if this was unsuccessful he stole. He was quite open about this, and said that in this he followed his father (also often in trouble), who had a motto 'why pinch pennies when there's tuppence at the side of you'. He also admitted that he was sometimes stupid about the use of the money he stole: for example, he might steal £15 because he was hard up for household payments, and then spend it all on drink. Discussion with the probation officer during the social inquiry process revealed that Stuart had astronomically high electricity bills, due to keeping the fires on all day for his young children.

As regards his social situation, Stuart was married with three young boys aged three, two and one. He said he didn't really get on with his wife and he 'would like her to leave'. If she did go, ideally he would like her to leave the boys behind, but practically he doubted whether he could manage in such a situation. The family lived in a new council flat, having been rehoused from their previous terrace house in the street due for demolition. Stuart had been unemployed for two years at the time of the offences, having left his last job because, he claimed, the firm did not provide adequate washing facilities at the end of the working day. The family income consisted only of Stuart's social security cheques and his wife's family allowance.

How would such a case be assessed in terms of risk of re-offending? As regards predisposing hazards the picture is a fairly bleak one: Stuart has as many as five previous convictions; is beyond the most crime-prone age but is still a fairly young man; has a short gap since his previous offence; and has committed these offences alone. As regards situational hazards, a chronic and recurrent shortage of money is obviously the main such hazard linked to offending; but another is the unresolved emotional situation with his wife, which among other things leads him to seek company (and, no doubt, spend money) outside the home (the planned group burglary seemed to have arisen from such contacts).

We have said that situational hazards are identified by social work methods in the individual case. It is important to point out at this stage that these hazards are also potentially susceptible to social work help, in a way that the predisposing hazards are not. In the case of Stuart, the identified situational hazards of finance, marital relationships and time occupancy outside the home could be subject to creative discussion and planning between report writer and offender (for example, as to whether planned budgeting and more careful use of money could reduce the impact of financial shortages). These are matters which link up with our discussion of 'needs' and 'resources', below.

As a final point, it is worth mentioning that an SIR which does not avoid looking seriously at the risk of re-offending may actually increase rather than diminish the report writer's authority and credibility with both the court and the offender. Also, it should not act to the offender's detriment so long as it is allied to a sensitive and thorough exploration of the needs resulting from the risks, and the resources available to deal with them.

Risk of damage to the offender and his family and friends consequential on offending or likely offending
It is important to recognize that there is more than one kind of risk that the report writer needs to consider. Risk of re-offending *by* the offender is an obvious topic; risk of offending-related damage *to* the offender and his family and friends is less obvious, but no less important from a social work perspective.

The risk of this kind of damage is generated either by the commission of the current offence, or by the possibility of future offending.

Risk of damage arising from the current offence itself can be very direct and immediate, as in a case of child abuse within the family where the offender's spouse and parental relationships are clearly likely to have been damaged. Risks from the current offence can also, however, arise more indirectly, for example from the understandable reaction of local communities to some kinds of offence committed in their midst; or from the incapacitating levels of guilt experienced by some offenders, particularly those appearing before the courts for the first time, about their own actions. In each of these cases, identification of the risk of damage requires a sensitive social-work-based awareness of the offender's reaction to his offence, and an awareness also of family relationships and/or local community networks. This can then lead to a linked discussion of needs, and of the resources available to deal with risk and need (see below).

It is important to stress that some risks of damage of this kind can arise even where the risk of re-offending is absent or very slight (an over-remorseful first-time offender is a good example). This emphasizes the point that the report writer should be alert to this kind of risk as well as to the more commonly identified risk of re-offending.

The second kind of risk of damage arises from the possibility of future offending. For example, in an interview a spouse might make it unambiguously clear that should the offender re-offend, she will not stay with him, even though they both want the relationship to continue if possible. Or again, a report writer might identify likely physical or psychological damage to an offender arising from a continuation of serious drink or drug-related offences. Once again, the identification of such risks is an important part of the report writer's task, and is linked to subsequent consideration of needs and resources; although in these instances, unlike the first set of cases identified, there is by definition a close link between risk of future re-offending and risk of damage.

Need

Social work values require the report writer to consider the personal and social needs of the offender (see Chapter 3). Nevertheless, 'need' is a notoriously difficult and slippery concept to handle. The main dangers are that, without a careful approach to the topic, almost anything can be defined as a 'need'; almost anyone can decide what another person 'needs'; and, in consequence, inappropriate intervention in the lives of others can be justified in the name of 'need'. Regrettably, Curnock and Hardiker do not avoid all of these pitfalls, operating as they do without any carefully defined concept of need. For example, in one of their case illustrations a youth described as 'a fairly stable young man' (and therefore presumably with few personal/social problems as usually understood) was nevertheless considered to have a 'need' for the 'shock' of detention centre 'because he had been able to go his own way for quite a while' (Curnock and Hardiker 1979, p.62).

This book is not the appropriate place for a general treatise on social and personal need (see Smith 1980). Nevertheless, we think that some controlling guidelines can be evolved which will help practitioners not to fall into the difficulties and dangers of a wholly unfocused and free-floating concept of 'need'. These guidelines fall into two main categories: the first links 'need' to the prior discussion of 'risk', while the second controls the concept of 'need' by taking as its starting-point the offender's own definition of need.

Need and risk

In the previous section it was seen that careful identification of 'risk' (of both types) often throws up a set of personal and social needs related either to risk of re-offending or to risk of damage. (For example, in the case of Stuart, possible needs in the areas of finance, marital relationship and time occupancy were identified.) Many SIRs have traditionally discussed offenders' needs in a rather general way, without specifically considering whether or not they are related to the kinds of risk we have identified. In our view, it is always essential for report writers to consider whether identified needs are or are not related to risk, and, if they are, to make clear the connection in the report.

An approach of this kind yields the following simple classification of personal/social need:

1 personal/social need related to risk of offending;
2 personal/social need related to risk of damage consequential on offending or likely offending;
3 personal/social need unrelated to either kind of risk.

The first two require no further discussion. The third kind of need has in practice often been included in SIRs, but in our view it is not appropriate to include information of this sort in the report since it is peripheral to the main concerns of the court, and hence not relevant material. However, in the social inquiry process more generally, need unrelated to risk certainly should be identified and dealt with by the report writer in a way which is appropriate and helpful given her social work responsibilities. An example known to one of the authors was where a mother was being interviewed about the court appearance of her two young teenage sons, and she raised anxieties concerning rehousing following the impending termination of her lease: this was dealt with, with the mother's agreement, by writing a letter to the local housing department.

An illustration of the importance of distinguishing carefully whether or not need is related to risk can be found in considering an article by Peter Raynor (1981) on the Pontypridd Day Training Centre. Raynor compared the expressed problems of clients in the centre (obtained on a self-report basis), with those perceived by probation officers and articulated in the SIRs on those clients.[9] The main types of problem identified by the clients were, in order of frequency: (i) employment, (ii) income, (iii) health, (iv) social relationships, and (v) accommodation. By contrast, analysis of the SIRs produced the following list of problems: (i) employment, (ii) family relationships, (iii) income, (iv) social relationships, and (v) lack of motivation. Clearly, there is some congruence between the two lists, but also an apparent difference of emphasis, with probation officers, but not clients, tending to stress family relationships and lack of motivation, while the clients raised health and accommodation problems which were less often mentioned by probation officers.

A conflicting result of this kind could have arisen because clients and probation officers held genuinely different views about what, in general, the clients' main problems and needs actually were (see further below); and this is how Raynor treats this particular result. But there is another possible interpretation, not considered by Raynor, which illustrates our earlier discussion. It might well be that the probation officers knew about, and were genuinely empathetic to, the clients' health problems, for example; but it might also be the case that they considered them to be of little or no relevance to the clients' past offending, future risk of offending, or future risk consequential on offending, and this was why health problems were excluded from the reports.

A careful consideration of the relationship between risk and need therefore certainly provides some control and clarification of the 'need' concept in social inquiry practice. However, this is not in itself sufficient to ensure that the 'need' concept is not used in an inappropriately wide way. For example, report writers who recommend that clients 'need' custody may often do so with explicit recognition of a perceived link to risk of re-offending. More generally, need related to risk (perhaps particularly risk of damage to the offender himself) can be defined in very paternalistic ways by the report writer, leading to the well recognized dangers of 'unbridled welfarism' which takes no account of the offender's own definition of the situation. Additional control of the need concept is therefore clearly required.

Starting with the client
In order to combat the dangers of an inappropriately imposed definition of client 'needs', we suggest it is important to take seriously the often-endorsed social work dictum of 'starting with the client'. That is, the client should be encouraged to indicate what he thinks his own needs are. This initial discussion will probably encompass needs both related and unrelated to risk, and the client's views will act as a check on the report writer's assumptions about client needs.

It was seen above that there are difficulties in accepting uncritically whatever the report writer chooses to identify as 'need'. If, as we are advocating, one always starts with clients' views, is there not an analogous problem in accepting uncritically whatever the client says about his need: as Raynor (1985, p.92) puts it, are we committed to 'a blind adherence to the first difficulty our client happens to mention?',

We think the answer to this is in the negative, though such an answer does not negate the advantage of starting with the client's own view. To explain the implications of this, some consideration of how needs are best identified is required. Discussing his Pontypridd study (see p.79), Raynor (1981, p.43) comments that:

> the fact that the men in this study were mostly able to produce comprehensive and useful assessments of their own problems and to contribute actively to the formulation of goals and programmes should not blind us to the fact that they had not done so before, although the problems were often of long standing.

What made the difference on this occasion was the setting or context (Raynor 1981, p.43):

> their achievement reflects the provision of an appropriate context, practical and effective methods, and an atmosphere of encouragement, support and some demand.

In short, the necessary setting in which a client can begin to identify his own needs is a collaborative one. Within such a setting, the parties will ideally engage in honest, open, and constructive discussion, from which a measure of agreement will be achieved. To safeguard against such agreements being merely collusive (for example, the report writer accepting the client's definition of need uncritically, for the sake of peace or work avoidance), the report writer should ensure that agreements are fully congruent with the best social work professionalism. Hence, we can suggest as one criterion for an acceptable definition of 'need' that if the offender and the report writer agree on the need, and the report writer is using social work skills and knowledge and operating within social work values, then the 'need' can be regarded as established.

However, even after the most constructive discussions, agreement about definitions of need will not always ensue. Should this occur, with needs which are related to risk (see above) then, whether it is the report writer who identifies a need with which the offender disagrees or vice versa, the important thing is that both views should be contained in the report, but in a way which clearly explains the differences and is not detrimental or damaging to the offender. This is a practical example of a point touched on earlier, namely that there are some unavoidable differences in power and situation between the report writer and the offender, but that nevertheless within this framework as collaborative, respectful and caring an approach as possible should be developed (see Chapters 2 and 3).

A collaborative approach of this kind is not only helpful in controlling inappropriate definitions of 'need' (by both report writer and offender); it also paves the way for a purposeful discussion of the kind of options that might be offered to the court at the sentencing stage, and, beyond that, it lays a sound basis for any future supervisory relationships which may ensue. For, as Raynor (1985, p.53) again puts it:

> Effective social work depends partly on compatibility between the help offered and the client's own view of his problems and goals. This will be difficult to achieve in programmes which allow little space for clients' points of view or for the negotiation of agreed objectives.

Need: a summary
This discussion of need has perhaps been a little complex, so it is worth restating the main points briefly. 'Need' is a slippery concept liable to abuse; to avoid this, some safeguards are necessary. In the context of SIR writing, we have suggested two main controlling safeguards. The first insists that the relationship between 'need' and 'risk' is always present in the report writer's mind; the second is that discussion of need should always begin with the client's own definition, and then proceed by collaborative discussion. While these safeguards may not eliminate all possible abuses of the 'need' concept, they will, we suggest, go far along the right road; and in any case, both safeguards are fully congruent with a focused SIR practice rooted in social work principles and values.

To illustrate the importance of these points, let us consider briefly some results from Stanley and Murphy's (1984) study of SIRs in Inner London. In this project, the researchers evolved a list of 'indicators of present needs for supervision', and then analysed the contents of nearly 1000 SIRs to ascertain what they said about such needs. The specific categories of need indication used by the researchers were: (i) having problems in functioning (including debt, lack of social skills, and 'problems of fulfilling a particular role in life'); (ii) being addicted to drink, drugs or gambling; (iii) having problems with relationships; (iv) having suffered recent crises (family, housing or employment); (v) having psychological problems; (vi) being subject to criminal influences; and (vii) affected by aspects of family pathology. Such a list would probably pass as uncontroversial in most probation offices. From our point of view a list such as this offers a valuable starting-point for the identification of need, but it is necessary, before finally including needs of these kinds in a report, to test ideas about 'having problems in functioning' etc. both against (i) the risk factor (both risk of re-offending and risk of damage), and (ii) the client's own view of his situation and needs.

There is one last point to make before we leave the areas of risk and need. At the end of Chapter 4, the value of beginning the SIR interviews with a discussion of current offence(s) and any previous offending was emphasized, and it was suggested that this helps to marshal and keep relevant the subsequent obtaining of social information. In the light of the discussion in this chapter, it can also be seen that beginning the interview by discussing offending also ensures a focus upon risk as a natural and logical topic to be developed at an appropriate point in the interview, and this in turn allows consideration of needs related to risk. Beginning the interview with offending thus both provides a helpful discipline for the report writer and, we would suggest, helps to achieve a relevant focus and an atmosphere in which risk and connected need can be discussed in a collaborative manner.

Resources

'Resources' is obviously a very different, and perhaps more down-to-earth, concept than is either 'risk' or 'need'. When dealing with risk, we considered risks posed by or to the offender and his family and friends, while 'need' also focused upon the offender. 'Resources' is a much more general idea. It gains its point as part of this chapter only if it is seen in very close relationship with identified risk and need, though it also looks forward to possible community options to be offered to the court (see Chapter 6).

The importance of considering resources as part of social inquiry practice was emphasized in Home Office Circular 18/1983, in which para. 5 states:

> it will be particularly helpful, when making recommendations, if the court is aware of the various non-custodial facilities which are available in the area. In recent years the probation service has made increasing use of local groups and activities in supervising offenders, and it is important that sentencers should be informed of these resources.

Despite such exhortation, it is, in our experience, rather rare to find any serious references to resources in discussions about SIR writing. Even Curnock and Hardiker (1979), from whom we have derived the helpful threefold categorization used in this chapter, devote very little space to the subject (see pp. 62-5). Moreover, Curnock and Hardiker's discussion of resources is inadequate on a number of grounds. In several of the cases discussed, 'resources' seems to be simply equated with and a synonym for a particular court disposal (for example, 'probation may be a positive resource in a case which might otherwise be discharged'); but this tells us little about what kind of activities the probation order is offering to meet identified risk and need. Secondly, Curnock and Hardiker seem to restrict the concept of resources to the individual probation officer involved, other recognized standard probation facilities such as hostels, or to the local 'medical, social and psychiatric services'; thus other less conventional resources in the wider community are not covered. Thirdly, Curnock and Hardiker comment that 'probation officers formulate their assessments within the context of available resources' (p. 62); this may be an accurate description of much local practice, but it runs the risk of seeing resources in over-restricted terms rather than looking creatively at how to mobilize resources positively to meet identified risks and needs.

How then should resources be considered? There are two general points to make before the details of this question can be considered. First, in the context of the SIR process, the consideration of resources is a highly individualized process: resources are considered strictly as they might contribute to helping with the identified needs, risks and personal situations of individual offenders. It is no good knowing about an alcoholics group and a fishing club if the offender has no drink problem and hates fishing. Secondly, in order to overcome the inadequacies which we have suggested in Curnock and Hardiker's approach to resources, it is essential for practitioners to develop both (i) a wider vision (or concept) of resources – that is, some lateral thinking about the idea of 'resources' which sees them in much wider terms than is often the case; and (ii) a good deal of detailed knowledge about resources in local areas. Perhaps paradoxically, unless this wider vision and detailed knowledge is available to practitioners, they will be unable to be fully helpful in the highly individualized process of considering resources specific to a particular person's risk and need.

An example of what we mean by a wider vision of resource identification concerns what might be called 'personal strengths'.[10] By this we mean the positive and life-enhancing aspects of the offender's personality, interests and social activities, and the extent to which people close to him (family, close friends, etc.) can support the offender and help to meet his identified needs. Indeed, we would argue that an identification of these 'personal strengths' should always occur in the SIR process along with the identification of risks and needs. Hence, when considering resources, the first question should always be how far the offender and his immediate family and friends have positive resources to offer to meet identified risks and needs.

What other resources might be available to a report writer in an individual case? This question will be considered under four headings: the probation service,[11] other statutory agencies, voluntary agencies, and informal networks and groups.

The probation service The most obvious resource is the report writer, who more often than not will be earmarked as the likely supervisor should the court make a supervisory disposal, with the assumption being made that all work on the case will be carried out by that supervisor. Such an assumption is unnecessarily restrictive, and inhibits the creative involvement of team colleagues. The local team has an important role to play in three respects: first, in sharing discussion of an SIR with the report writer so as to maximize creative thinking about resources which might be available to meet identified needs and risks; secondly, in themselves acting as resources in the event of a supervisory disposal, assuming here that different members of the team have different special skills, experience, and interests; and, thirdly, in collaboratively constructing (and keeping up-to-date) an index of local resources outside the probation service (see further below), upon which report writers can draw. Over and above the local team, the probation service has other resources. There are of course the recognized standard facilities such as hostels and day centres, and many probation areas have created specific projects and facilities to meet needs in their local areas, for example a workshop for unemployed offenders or an alcohol group. Another important resource is the probation service's pool of voluntary associates. Most services have also created an information bank for officers and teams, detailing resources at county and national level, though we suspect that many such information services are under-used by local teams.

Other statutory agencies These will include, of course, medical and social services but may also, in an individual case, involve the education service (including further education), the housing department (especially where it has special housing schemes), the recreation department, and possibly the police (for example, in some areas the police run motor-cycle projects for young offenders convicted of taking vehicles). With all these, there is again a danger of under-use through lack of knowledge, which could be avoided by regular liaison and the creation in local probation teams of a good index of local resources (see p.85).

Voluntary agencies This is obviously not the place to provide an exhaustive list of voluntary agencies, which will in any event vary with local conditions and situations. It is important to note, however, that the voluntary sector ranges from large national agencies such as Dr Barnardo's or NACRO to small and usually more specialized groups such as Alcoholics Anonymous and Homestart, or groups with a purely local focus. Once again the key to the best use of such resources lies in the collection of appropriate information so that it is readily available to report writers.

Both in respect of these agencies, and the statutory agencies mentioned above, it will usually be important for the probation service to be prepared to be reciprocal in its dealings: that is, to be willing to act as a resource for that other agency where appropriate, for example through training inputs or specialist advice.

Informal networks and groups The discussion so far has concentrated on resources which, because of their funding, status, and/or formal constitution, are quite easily identifiable in local communities. Less visible from a distance, but very important nevertheless in considering resources, are more informal links and strengths within communities. These might include, for example, particular individuals within a community who might be in a position to assist a given offender. These individuals would include people able to help an offender with, for example, a recreational activity (in some parts of the country 'befriending schemes' exist to link offenders and others in this way); but they would also include those people described by Abrams (1978) as 'caring agents' – that is, people in the local community able to offer help and care beyond the norm. Ex-offenders, either as individuals or in group situations, may also be able to offer a valuable resource to current offenders.[12] Beyond the individual level, there is of course a whole range of local community groups who may be able to offer appropriate resources in an individual case. Good use of this informal range of resources requires that the local probation team knows its communities really well, and is prepared to spend time in them (and not just through luncheon clubs!).

This discussion of resources can now be drawn together in a series of necessary practical steps for the report writer, as follows:

1   identify risk, and risk-related need;
2   in considering resources, begin by looking at the 'personal strengths' of the offender and his family and friends, and how far these can in themselves meet risks and needs;
3   in considering wider resources, first free oneself of the idea that the report writer has to have all the answers; in particular look to the strengths of team colleagues;
4   consider how the resources identified in (2) and (3) can best be supported and supplemented by other resources in the probation service, other statutory and voluntary agencies, and informal networks and groups.

The importance of integration
We have considered 'risks', 'needs' and 'resources' separately, but it is important to stress that report writers should deal with them as a coherent whole. The three are intimately connected: for example, the more one refines one's consideration of risk, the more one is able to clarify a consideration of risk-related need, and to identify appropriate resources. Similarly, the more one has a wide vision of resources and a detailed understanding of local provision, the less likely one is to fail to notice particular types of risk-related need in an offender just because one knows there would be no resources to deal with them anyway.

Just as 'risks', 'needs' and 'resources' have to be seen as an integrated whole, so too the whole consideration of the offender's future prospects, as discussed in this chapter, has to be carefully linked to other aspects of the SIR process. Thus, the discussion of the offence and offending history should lead on naturally to considering the offender's future prospects through 'risks', 'needs' and 'resources'; and this in turn will point the way to thinking about the kind of suggestions which might be made to the court about possible disposals (see Chapter 6).

A case example
To try to illustrate some features of the discussion in this chapter and the previous one, we have rewritten the report for Mr Green (Case C, Chapter 1, p.12) in an attempt to show how the approach to SIR writing which we have outlined might affect the finished product (see also Chapter 6, p.98, for the conclusion of the rewritten report on Mr Green, and the Appendix for rewritten versions of the reports on Mr Bishop and Mr Davenport (Cases A and B in Chapter 1)).[13]

Name: Brian Green (aged 20)
Offences:
1 Burglary
2 Theft
3 Obtain money by deception
Information relevant to offending and previous offences:

1 The three current charges are all connected. Mr Green told me that he went to the estate agent's office posing as a first-time house buyer. He was given a set of keys and went to the house, where he removed some ornaments. The house was unoccupied and had hardly any furniture in it since it was waiting to be sold. When he tried to sell these items a few days later, somebody recognized one of them and informed the police. Mr Green said that at the time the offence was committed (about two months ago) he and his family were very short of money. He decided that he did not want to ask either his or his wife's parents to help them out, since in his opinion he had relied upon them too much in the past. He has been in custody since his arrest.

2 The court will be aware that Mr Green's criminal record makes very disturbing reading. He was taken into care at the age of eleven for his involvement in group offences of theft and burglary; he has continued to commit similar offences since then at regular intervals, and has been sentenced to detention centre, borstal and finally prison.

3 Since his release from an 18-month prison sentence in April 1981, Mr Green has spent his longest period out of custody for many years. After the expiry of his young prisoner licence, and apart from today's hearing, Mr Green has been before the court on two other occasions. The first was for theft of meat, for which he was sentenced to 120 hours community service. The second, for handling stolen goods, resulted in the imposition of a suspended sentence. Today's appearance thus puts him in breach of that last disposal, and he still has 20 hours of his CSO to complete as well.

4 Mr Green and I spent some time talking about his criminal career. He was able to recognize that up to his CSO offence all previous crimes had been motivated by greed and the desire for material gain. It also seemed to me that, from his descriptions of these earlier offences, he must have got a considerable thrill and excitement from his participation. The CSO, suspended sentence and now the current offence seem to have had different motives; namely money in order to provide for his family. It is significant in this context that Mr Green has committed the last three sets of offences alone. Nevertheless, the consistency and frequency of Mr Green's offending pattern means that there is a great danger of attracting the description of 'old lag' at a very early and still formative age, and of being dealt with accordingly.

5 Mr Green's early contact with social workers has not been described in very optimistic ways in the social services records I have read. However his more recent statutory contacts with the probation service have been

reasonably good. For a young man with such an institutionalized background and the feelings towards authority figures that often suggests, Mr Green has been surprisingly consistent in maintaining contact, and has often sought his probation officers out voluntarily when particular difficulties have arisen. The Community Service organizer has submitted good reports about his attendance and the work he has done, especially on the individualized part of the order.

Current situation and future prospects:

6 Having married last year, Mr and Mrs Green now have a seven-month-old son; Mrs Green is expecting another child in the late autumn. They obtained an old council house when they married and most of Mr Green's time has been spent decorating and refurbishing it. Mr Green is unemployed and in receipt of £58 per week supplementary benefit: rent is paid direct. In addition his wife receives £4.50 per week child benefit. They have no other sources of income, and the normal outgoings with no outstanding debts.

7 Given Mr Green's well-established pattern of behaviour, and the financial need motivating his current offending, there is clearly a high risk that Mr Green will continue to offend. At our meetings for the preparation of this report Mr Green has been emphatic that his latest period on remand has brought home to him that – given his changed circumstances as a father and a husband – this is no longer a way of life that he wishes to follow. He is realistic enough to recognize that his avowed good intentions have to be matched by action and quite difficult and demanding changes in his behaviour. He is also aware that further offending and the consequent periods of imprisonment would damage his domestic relationships, and seriously threaten his attempts to create some stability for himself in what has hitherto been a volatile and disrupted life.

8 Mr Green identified a need to improve his behaviour, and he told me that he had not been given the opportunity to do this in the past. I suggested to him that the outside world may well think he had been given ample opportunity to do so. Be that as it may, there are ways in which he could be helped to strive to change his seemingly instinctive response to financial hardship by offending. Such ways would be very demanding in requiring him to confront those areas in himself that are resistant to change. He would also participate in a group in which he could expect to be confronted by other group members further along the path to change than he is. Mr Green is intelligent enough to understand that attempts at change are long and slow processes and are often punctuated by setbacks. Nevertheless he still expresses a commitment to a proposed course of action which will make high demands upon him. His wife has also committed herself fully to supporting him in such a venture. They both know that if he chooses the 'easy way' of continued criminality, their relationship would be of short duration only.

Notes

1 However, most justice model theorists allow a limited and subsidiary role to other factors in determining amount: for the clearest discussion see von Hirsch (1986).

2 For criticisms of various kinds see Clarke (1978); Walker (1980, Chapter 2; 1985, Chapter 8); Hudson (1987).

3 Curnock and Hardiker's book is part of a general series of works by Pauline Hardiker which are both complex and controversial. It is not necessary to explore these issues here: for a brief assessment of Hardiker's work see Bottoms and McWilliams (1986, pp.261-7).

4 There is also an unfortunate tendency in Curnock and Hardiker to confuse the concepts of 'risk' and of 'tariff': see, on this, Paley and Leeves (1982).

5 These factors are probabilistic, and are based on past experience gained from studying fairly large groups of offenders; they will, therefore, not necessarily determine the outcome for any particular individual offender in the future. For discussions of these kinds of factors with varying groups of offenders in England see, for example, Nuttall (1977, Chapter 2); Philpotts and Lancucki (1979, Chapter 3); Bottoms and McClintock (1973, Chapter 11).

6 This factor is strongly in evidence if all male and female offenders are considered together. However, this result is clearly related to the fact that unselected groups of male offenders usually have significantly more previous convictions than do similar groups of female offenders. In one small study in Cambridge, when this difference in previous convictions was controlled for, gender had no independent effect on reconviction (Farrington and Morris 1982, p.243). However, in the larger national study by Philpotts and Lancucki (1979, Table 3.1, p.15), women still had a substantially lower reconviction rate when previous convictions were controlled for.

7 This factor has been shown to be important by both Nuttall (1977) and Bottoms and McClintock (1973). The reason for the finding has not yet been established.

8 On burglary and robbery, see Philpotts and Lancucki (1979, pp.14-17); on arson, see Soothill and Pope (1973).

9 It should be noted that Raynor's terminology in this article refers to 'problems' rather than 'needs', but we do not consider that this affects the point which we make in relation to Raynor's interpretation of the data.

10 This again draws on the work of Paul Brearley (1982, pp. 82 ff.).

11 For simplicity, we have concentrated here on the probation service rather than social services departments; but similar points apply in the context of social services departments' work with juvenile offenders.

12 We should perhaps make clear that we are not suggesting here anything other than a minimal formal oversight by the agency of these 'offender-other' relationships.

13 We had no details of these cases other than those contained in the original reports themselves (see Chapter 1). Where, therefore, there seemed to be important information missing from the original reports, we have had to invent this detail for the purpose of these illustrations.

6 Community options for the court

This chapter addresses the central issue of how report writers should make suggestions to the court about the sentence. But before this issue can be reached, it is necessary to consider the report writer's preparatory discussions with the offender.

Discussing what happens next
In our proposed framework for social inquiry practice, the report writer has already discussed fully with the offender his offending behaviour, relevant social information and future prospects. As she reaches the end of the interview(s), the report writer inevitably has to confront the fact that the offender will be appearing in court very soon, and that a suggestion for disposal will be expected by the court.

We suggest that the same style of collaborative sharing should again be adopted as this part of the interview is reached. That is, the hierarchical examination mode of social work practice should so far as possible be avoided (see Chapter 2), and the report writer should again start with the client's view, though not necessarily share it ultimately (see Chapter 5).

The task for the report writer and client at this point should be *to think collaboratively about what kind of activities might best help the offender strive to eliminate or reduce the offending-related risks, and to meet the risk-related needs, previously identified* (see Chapter 5). In that context, one can reasonably begin by asking the defendant to say what he would see as most helpful and constructive, although in the ensuing discussion the report writer might well make suggestions to the defendant, and/or supply information about the content of various sentences, or of particular facilities such as hostels or drug programmes.

Such a discussion must be so conducted as to ensure that difficult or unpalatable issues are not avoided by either party. Hence the report writer, while fully maintaining her care and respect for the offender, must not allow him to evade the reality of recent offending, or of future risks of offending. Squarely facing these issues, the two parties can then appropriately consider what consequences the variety of possible disposals (including imprisonment) could have for the defendant and his family. In this way, the defendant becomes an active participant in the process of thinking about his future, rather than a passive recipient of the report writer's suggestions and expertise as to disposal.

In considering agency-based disposals, this discussion should always explore what, for example, 'being on probation' or 'getting community service' might actually mean in practice for this particular offender. In the case of probation or supervision orders, such an exploration is increasingly recognized as good practice, for, as Raynor (1980) says:

> more attention to the role of social inquiry work in exploring the basis for future help would lead to better and more purposeful supervision.

In the case of community service, present SIR practice too rarely explores the likely tasks and how they might be relevant to the offender's risks and needs. Such an omission can scarcely be defended if 'respect for the offender' is seen as a core social work value, and if (as is legally the case) consent to the making of the order is required. A revision of practice of this kind would require much closer links between report writers and area community service organizers.

Some writers have suggested that the demise of 'expert diagnosis and treatment' (see Chapter 2) requires that recommendations by probation officers in SIRs should necessarily carry the offender's consent if they are to be legitimate (Raynor 1980; Bottoms and McWilliams 1979). In our approach, custodial and suspended custodial recommendations are almost always precluded (see Chapter 3), and probation and community service orders legally require consent, so for adult defendants the issue is a live one only for recommendations for fines, compensation, attendance centres, discharge and deferred sentences. That being so, the issue is scarcely of major importance, but our approach to it would be similar to that relating to the identification of 'need' in the previous chapter. That is, suggestions for disposals by the report writer should preferably carry the offender's consent, and should in any case be developed using social work knowledge, skills, and values; but where consent from the offender is not forthcoming this should be explained in the report in a way which is not detrimental to him. We would, however, wish to emphasize the importance of consent (where applicable) being *informed* consent; that is, the offender must be clearly aware of what it is that he is actually likely to experience when he consents to a particular proposed disposal.

'Alternatives to Custody'

At this point in the discussion, we move away for a moment from day-to-day practice to tackle a very important conceptual and organizational issue which has vital practical implications. This issue concerns the much-used phrase 'alternatives to custody'.

Successive crises of prison overcrowding since the mid-1960s have led to an increasingly urgent search, on the part of Home Office civil servants and others, for credible 'alternatives to custody' – hence the creation (for offenders over 17) of suspended sentences (1967), community service orders (1972), day training centres (1972), partly suspended sentences (1977) and special-requirement 'enhanced' probation orders (1982).[1] In the probation service, these developments have occurred simultaneously with the loss of faith in the treatment ideal, so that rather naturally the service tended to adopt 'providing alternatives to custody' as a new overarching goal (McWilliams 1986). This book, focusing as it does on SIRs, and refusing as it does to recommend custody, might be thought to be enthusiastic about such an approach.

In fact, we believe there are very serious difficulties about this whole impetus, especially when the matter is considered from a social work point of view. We would list five principal problems.

First, there is a problem about language. The concept 'alternatives to custody' appears linguistically to give primacy to imprisonment as a punishment, and to view other disposals simply as alternatives or variations from it. Yet there is no particular reason why imprisonment should be accorded this primacy (and statistically, more than three-fifths of adult indictable offenders are not given imprisonment, either immediate or suspended). As Speller (1986, p. 137) has put it:

> The language needs to be changed. Just as changes in racist and sexist language can lead to changes in perception and practice, so can changes in the language of criminal justice.

Secondly, and related to the first point, the use of the phrase 'alternatives to custody' emphasizes only the *negative* dimension of the community disposal (that is, what it is an alternative to), rather than anything which it might creatively and positively achieve in its own right.

Thirdly, the concept 'alternatives to custody' tends to lead to community-based agencies creating 'packages' which are designed above all to be, in the jargon phrase, 'credible alternatives'. 'Credible', in this context, usually means simply 'acceptable to the court', and, since community agencies often do not know exactly what courts really want, there sometimes ensues a rather desperate search for any set of arrangements which can be presented to courts in suitably rigorous terms as a 'real alternative' (very frequent attendances at projects, instant breach action for any failure, intensive surveillance of the client, etc.). Thus, social work practitioners are in effect encouraged to meet the needs (or perceived needs) of the court, and the identified risk-related needs of the defendant can sometimes get forgotten.

Fourthly, the processes described above can too easily lead to unintended consequences. The literature of 'alternatives to custody' is replete with examples of situations where courts use the so-called 'alternatives' as alternatives to other non-custodial options rather than to custody itself (Bottoms 1981; Pease 1985; Bottoms 1987). Indeed, nationally the use of imprisonment by the courts has actually increased during the decade which introduced community service orders in England and Wales (1975-85). This is not an inevitable trend, and in some local areas there have been significant reductions in custody following on the creation of 'alternatives to custody' for juvenile offenders (Richardson 1987). Nevertheless, there is a danger that, at least in some areas, as many people will be sent to prison as before the introduction of the 'alternatives to custody', while others will receive the 'alternative' who would not otherwise have gone to prison. Thus, overall, the total level of social control over offenders would be increased (Cohen 1985).

Fifthly, and flowing from the previous point, the 'alternatives to custody' development can lead to a general movement of disposals 'up-tariff'. Specific examples of this could be the overshadowing of probation by community service (because the latter is seen as more of a 'real alternative'); and the promotion of 'special requirements' in probation orders (Criminal Justice Act 1982, Schedule 11), with a consequent devaluing of the 'ordinary' probation order, to the point where it can sometimes be regarded as suitable only for low-tariff offenders, despite Court of Appeal guidance to the contrary.[2]

In the light of these five points, we think that probation services and social services departments might well consider abandoning the language and implied practice of 'alternatives to custody', and instead might begin to present to courts the idea of 'community options'. Each community option would then have equal merit and could be advocated in its own right in terms of its own positive attributes and potential benefits for the defendant and society.

This conceptual change would also have the important consequence of clarifying, in probation and social services, the respective positive attributes of different community options. This process should also enable individual report writers to be clearer and more focused about the reasons why, in their particular local context, they are recommending one community option rather than another in the individual case they are reporting upon.

Making suggestions to the court

Most report writers, if asked how they end their reports, would unhesitatingly say 'with a recommendation to the court'.

This idea is much more problematic than is generally assumed. The difficulties were pointed out more than 25 years ago by the Streatfeild Committee, as part of its general concern to distinguish clearly between the roles of the sentencer and those who write different kinds of report (medical, prison, SIR, etc.) for the court (see Chapters 2 and 3). The writer of an SIR, said the committee:

> should never give his opinion in a form which suggests that it relates to all the considerations in the court's mind. *It is not a recommendation ...* (para. 346) [emphasis added]

Here the Committee clearly identified a recommendation as taking into account all relevant considerations before the court, including the public interest, general deterrence, and so on. We believe they were right to do so, and we further believe that many of the difficulties of subsequent years (notably the 'realism/credibility' issue – see Chapter 1) stem from a failure to recognize this simple point. Unfortunately the Home Office compounded the difficulties by using the word 'recommendation' routinely in the Home Office Circulars from 1974 to 1983;[3] and the term still appears, albeit in a changed context, in Home Office Circular 92/1986.[4] In our view, this is a serious mistake: the term 'recommendation' should *never* be used, for the reasons given long ago by the Streatfeild Committee.

Those who have found difficulty with the concept of a recommendation in the SIR have, over the years, proffered various alternative terms concerning the conclusion of the report. The three main alternative concepts suggested have been 'professional opinion', 'assessment' and 'offer'.

The Streatfeild Committee itself spoke of 'opinions', clearly meaning 'professional opinions'. These 'opinions' were to relate to 'only one of the possible considerations in the court's mind' (para. 346), namely, 'the likely effect on the offender's criminal career of probation or some other specified form of sentence' (para. 335 (c)).

The difficulty with this formulation, of course, is that report writers generally are unable to offer decisive advice on this particular matter (see Chapter 2). This renders the concept of a 'professional opinion' a difficult one to sustain in the SIR context; a point that is reinforced when one considers analogies with other professional opinions. The advice that the probation officer or social worker has to offer to the court clearly cannot carry the same force as, for example, the professional opinion of a hospital specialist on a patient's heart, a tax barrister on company tax liability, or a civil engineer on the structural state of a bridge.

The Central Council of Probation and After-Care Committees (CCPC) (1981) suggested that the term 'recommendation' should be dropped and that 'assessment' should replace it. However, it is very unclear exactly what the Council had in mind in advocating this change. But the Council did want assessments always to be 'realistic', and it complained of reports which contained no 'assessment', and 'thus fail to be of any help to the courts' (!) (para. 16). In general, the Council's proposal seemed to be simply a cosmetic name-change but with a rider seeking increased 'realism'.

At about the same time, Raynor (1980) suggested that, following a process of negotiation between officer and defendant, a conclusion could be reached on a form of 'contractual sentencing' which would carry the defendant's consent. This conclusion:

> should be *offered* to the court as a plausible alternative to the retributive tariff sentence, not *recommended* as an expertly selected treatment based on a scientific diagnosis.

Raynor's concept of an 'offer' certainly avoids the difficulty of all-inclusiveness implied by the term 'recommendation'. Nevertheless, in his framework the offer concept is tied closely to a concept of 'contractual sentencing' which is difficult to support. The problems with the concept are first, that the language of contract ('offer', 'acceptance', 'enforcement', etc.) simply does not translate well into the criminal court setting (what rights can the defendant enforce under the contract?); and, secondly, the concept runs the grave risk of confusing what might be legally enforceable requirements of a court order (probation etc.) with much more informal understandings arrived at between defendant and report writer about activities which might be undertaken in the course of a suggested order.

Our own alternative proposal is to speak of *community options* being *suggested* to the court. We see two major advantages which would flow if this terminology were to replace the term 'recommendation'. First, 'community options' being 'suggested' clearly do not pretend to include or take into account all the considerations germane to sentencing, while at the same time the potential pitfalls presented by the terms 'professional opinion' and 'offer' are avoided. Secondly, the use of the term 'options' clearly allows inclusion of more than one sentencing possibility for the court to consider, in contradistinction to traditional practice which has tended to 'recommend' just one sentence.

Our preference for the term 'community options' was evolved during the RSDO courses (we had originally favoured 'offers', following Raynor, but came to prefer 'options'). We were therefore pleased to see the term appearing in Home Office Circular 92/1986 under the heading 'review of sentencing options'. Unfortunately, the circular went on to confuse the issue by saying that, although the probation officer should make a 'review of sentencing options' (defined as 'a consideration of how far particular measures are likely to encourage an offender not to offend in the future, and a consideration of their effect on the offender and his or her family'), nevertheless, 'if a probation officer feels able to make a specific *recommendation*' [emphasis added] she should do so. As noted above, we would avoid this term. Rather, where a report writer considered that, from the point of view of a social work report committed to maximize the offender's human possibilities (see Chapter 3), just one possible option stood out, it should be referred to as a 'preferred option'.

As implied in the previous paragraph, in carrying out and presenting her review of options for the court, the report writer must again use social work knowledge and skills, within a framework of social work values. This was very well stated in Home Office Circular 18/1983 (though using the language of 'recommendations'):

> The purpose of such a recommendation, offered by a probation officer as an officer of the court, is to assist the judge or magistrates in deciding what is the best way of dealing with the offender. It will be one of a number of factors which [the court] must take into account ... *The particular value of such a recommendation is that it takes account of knowledge and experience gained from social work. Furthermore, the probation officer may be the only person connected with the case who had met the defendant in a comparatively informal setting.* As a result of professional training and dealing with a wide range of offenders, an

experienced probation officer is equipped to understand and interpret a defendant's attitude and disposition. (paras 2-3) [emphasis added]

On the RSDO courses, and the practice flowing from them, many probation officers found the concept of suggesting community options to the court, from a social-work-based perspective, a very helpful (and sometimes liberating) idea. Extensive discussions about the practice implications of the concept established three key points of procedure. First, the concept does not imply that the report writer should include a list of all available disposals,[5] nor should she feel obliged to go through the advantages and disadvantages of every available sentence; the task is rather to suggest to the court those options which properly arise from a social-work-based SIR process. Secondly, it is not of course necessary (though it is permissible) to suggest more than one option: if the social-work-based SIR process points to only one conclusion as being in the offender's own best interests (see Chapter 3), that should be put forward as the sole 'community option'. Thirdly, some officers found it helpful to head the last section of their reports with the phrase 'community options' (or their own equivalent): among other things, this has the practical advantage of making it clear that one is not in the business of recommending custodial sentences.

As a practical illustration of what is meant by this approach, we can now include the final section of a rewritten version of the report on Brian Green (see Chapter 5, p.88, for the first part of this rewritten report):

Community options open to the court:
9   Mr Green is the first to recognize that the likely outcome of today's hearing will be a custodial sentence. While it is clear that, for its duration, such a sentence will ensure that Mr Green does not commit offences, it is unlikely to have any positive long-term effect upon him. He has done previous 'time' with little trouble, indeed knows all the informal rules for getting through a custodial sentence as easily as possible. Another such sentence would remove him from the opportunity to demonstrate that he can act in a sustained and responsible way as a young father and husband. In terms of his own attempted development towards maturity, such a sentence would have no real effect. If the court does feel able to consider that in the long term an alternative course of action could be more fruitful, three possibilities come to mind.
10   The first is for consideration to be given to a long Community Service Order. The reports from the organizer suggest that he does perform tasks well. But while it is true that his personal placement work has been

especially good, I do not think that the kinds of demands and opportunities needed by Mr Green if he is to be diverted from further criminality are as forthcoming from CSO as from other community options.

11 The second possibility is to take Mr Green at his word and, without any statutory support, defer sentence for six months in the hope that he would demonstrate his ability to stay out of trouble.

12 The third possibility would be to offer statutory supervision in order that Mr Green could undertake some of the work outlined in paragraph 8. Such supervision would include his attendance on an offending behaviour course run by the probation service, as well as regular meetings with himself and his wife to help with any emotional and material difficulties presented by the imminent birth of their second child and their concerted attempts at bringing up a young family. Mrs Green has expressed her willingness to be involved in these meetings, and her commitment to them. This third option would put the sincerity of Mr Green's intentions to the test in the most demanding manner, and for that reason I think it the most likely of the three options to succeed.

Some issues of practice
Four issues of practice, arising out of the approach suggested above, are worth some additional comment. They are: how one makes positive suggestions; ruling out options; whether it is ever right to omit options altogether; and the importance of commenting on custody.

Making positive suggestions
It is very important that the section on 'community options' should flow coherently from the preceding parts of the report, with their emphasis on offending behaviour and on risks, needs and resources. Any positive suggestions made for disposals must be congruent with such an analysis, and must be as specific as possible about how the disposal would be undertaken, so that the court has before it a clear indication of the activities to be pursued by the defendant if the option is selected by the court.[6]

But, within this framework, what criteria should guide the report writer in her choice of options, and especially of a preferred option, to present to the court? In Chapter 2, we rejected Giller's test of aiming at 'the least restrictive sanction in keeping with the severity of the offence', since (among other things) this seemed to turn the SIR into a plea of mitigation. Nevertheless, Giller clearly has a point in emphasizing that report writers should not suggest major social work interventions in offenders' lives for trivial offences.

Earlier in this chapter, it was argued that the discussions between report writer and offender, if they followed the paths we have recommended, would lead naturally to a collaborative consideration of what kind of activities might best help the offender to strive to eliminate or reduce offending-related risks, and to meet risk-related needs. It would also seem to follow that similar considerations should be the focus of the report writer's presentation of community options to the court. A good way of expressing this point, which also takes into account Giller's anxieties about excessive social work interventions, is to be found in the recent DHSS (1987) practice guide. According to the guide, a preferred community option:

> should aim at diverting the offender as effectively as possible from further crime ... with the minimum degree of intervention in the offender's life. (para. 101)[7]

We must, however, add one important rider to this point. In Chapter 2, we rejected Streatfeild's suggestion that report writers should include 'information relevant to the court's consideration of how the defendant's criminal career may be checked', on the grounds that no such information existed in a clear or specific form, and that this suggestion adopted a falsely scientific view of the potential control of human behaviour. Does not the above test reintroduce precisely the same problem?

In our view, it should not. We are not suggesting that skills or knowledge exist which would enable report writers to say whether disposal X would be more likely to reduce recidivism than disposal Y. Thus, any positive suggestion for a community option cannot guarantee success in the matter of re-offending, and this can be acknowledged in the report. What we are suggesting, however, is that the social work value of hope for the future impels the report writer to look for and suggest to the court some constructive options for the future, based on collaboratively identified achievable change relating to risk and risk-related need (see Chapter 5)[8] but with the minimum necessary degree of intervention in the offender's life.

Ruling out options

It will sometimes be appropriate for a report writer to comment specifically on why certain court disposals are not being put forward as community options. Examples would be where a defendant's current financial obligations would make the imposition of a fine or compensation counter-productive and perhaps likely to lead to imprisonment for default; or where the defendant's domestic or physical circumstances would make it very difficult to fulfil the requirements of a community service order.

Much less straightforward than these cases is the issue of ruling out agency-based community options on grounds such as present attitude, or criminal and social history (including past responses to supervision). It would seem that in the past such matters have often inhibited report writers from suggesting supervisory disposals. This was dramatically illustrated in the research by Stanley and Murphy (1984) in Inner London, where nearly two-thirds of all SIRs examined described the offender as being in need of some kind of supervision, yet more than half of this group were deemed inappropriate candidates for probation. The main reasons for this were as follows:

1 the report described 'contra-indicators' to supervision (of which the most important were having an adverse attitude to supervision or being considered unlikely to succeed under supervision);
2 the subject had 'several previous convictions';
3 the subject's problems were 'deep-seated', or related to addiction to drugs or alcohol (especially the latter).

Stanley and Murphy (1984, p.34) not unreasonably commented that the implication seemed to be that:

> probation officers were directing their recommendations for supervision not only towards offenders with short or non-existent criminal records, but also towards those whose needs were perhaps more immediate and easier to meet, at the expense of those with longer-lasting difficulties and criminal records.

Stanley and Murphy go on, not surprisingly, to conclude that the Inner London social inquiry practice manifested 'definite limits' in the efficacy of reports in diverting offenders from custody (p.36). We would say that many or most of the justifications offered for ruling out supervision in the London sample are not consistent with the kind of social-work-based inquiry practice outlined in this book, and indeed avoid the proper responsibilities of a social work agency.[9]

Omitting options
Should there ever be a complete absence of community options at the end of a report? Theoretically the answer to this question is perhaps 'no'. But, as argued in Chapter 3 apropos very serious offenders such as armed bank robbers, there is in practice very little point in suggesting options in cases of this gravity. This is part of what we can only describe as the 'messiness of practice' (that is, it is not

always sensible to follow theoretically correct procedures).

We do however wish very emphatically to say that the complete omission of options should be used very sparingly indeed, and only in cases of great gravity. This is because such an omission is clearly a signal to the court that a custodial disposal is regarded as inevitable, and we do not think such signals should be given lightly (cf. Roberts and Roberts 1982). To illustrate this, it may be helpful to look again at case example D (Mr Jenkins) in Chapter 4. The concluding part of the report in that case, which we omitted in Chapter 4, reads as follows.

Conclusion:
18   The eight-month delay in this case, whilst harrowing and unsettling for the defendant, has had the virtue of giving him the time to come to terms with his offending behaviour, fully acknowledge his guilt, and begin the process of personal adjustment and reorganization. Given Mr Jenkins's genuine remorse, I would respectfully suggest to the court that to imprison him at this stage would serve no useful purpose, and seriously hinder his process of rehabilitation. It is clear that Mr Jenkins is not a sophisticated criminal: he is a naive and simple man, whose family background has ill-equipped him for the demands of an adult emotional life. Given what he has already lost, the experience of custody would be literally unbearable for this man; it is not too dramatic to suggest that he is likely to suffer a fresh breakdown, and make further attempts on his life, in the event of imprisonment.
19   Accordingly, I would respectfully ask the court to give the most serious consideration to a probation disposal, notwithstanding the gravity of these offences. Besides acknowledging the work that Mr Jenkins has already done to break away from his past, Mr Jenkins feels that such an order would allow him to continue the exploration of his offending behaviour, which he has experienced as particularly helpful. He is willing to commit himself to supervision, feeling that it would provide the opportunity for him to

(a)   discuss and begin to resolve his confused feelings about his family and past
(b)   free himself up to develop other options for his future
(c)   provide support and encouragement for his resolve to keep out of further such trouble, and
(d)   facilitate putting him in touch with any social or medical resources locally.

What is of note here is that despite the obvious gravity of the offences, the report writer did not shy away from suggesting a community option, and indicating how it would work in practice. In the event, the offender received a sentence of five years' imprisonment, but no adverse comment on the SIR was made by the judge.

Commenting on custody
It will also be noted that, in the above example, paragraph 8 comments fully on the possible consequences of imprisonment from a social work perspective (see also paragraph 9 in the report on Mr Green). In our view, these are appropriate comments, for it is a legitimate and indeed necessary part of a social work report to bring to the court's attention any likely counter-productive effects of imprisonment on the offender and his family. Some report writers have argued against such a practice on the grounds that it might put into the court's mind the possibility of custody in a case where the court was not considering it; we find this argument unconvincing, since courts are clearly aware of their sentencing powers, and in any case we doubt whether SIRs have the degree of influence that such a proposition implies.[10]

Recapitulation: and credibility revisited
We have now completed our outline of a suggested framework for social inquiry practice for individual report writers. It is worth briefly re-emphasizing the point made in Chapter 5, namely that our suggestions should be seen as an integrated whole. For clarity of exposition we have dealt separately with the three elements of information relevant to offending, information relevant to future prospects, and community options for the court; but of course in daily practice all three aspects have to be dealt with together, and the degree of integration between the three should be very great.

At the end of Chapter 3 we posed a major question, as follows:

> Can a form of SIR practice be developed which is faithful to the core values of social work, and truly uses social work knowledge and skills; which genuinely minimizes the 'hierarchical examination' element of the SIR; which eschews direct or indirect custodial recommendations; and yet which does not lose credibility with the courts on the grounds of lack of realism?

We have tried to answer this question in the affirmative, and we hope that the detailed analysis in this and the previous two chapters has met all the elements in the question save the last. It remains, therefore, for us to readdress the issue of 'credibility' in the light of our analysis. It is of course often difficult to know, from a report writer's perspective, what exactly is in the mind of a given bench or judge; and one must recognize that sentencers themselves vary not a little in their views and attitudes. Hence there are obviously difficulties about knowing what produces 'credibility' in any general way. Nevertheless, we think it not unreasonable to suggest that some of the elements of our proposed framework for SIR practice are of the kind which will (or should) carry credibility with sentencers.[11] The main such elements are as follows:

1 *Offending behaviour.* We have argued that explicit attention needs to be given by report writers to offending behaviour (present and past), and that wherever possible the prosecution's view of the offence should be obtained, for the purposes of more informed offence-based discussion with the defendant (Chapter 4). Such a practice focuses squarely upon the court's main concerns, and does not seek to evade the negative, difficult or unpalatable aspects of the defendant's behaviour.

2 *Risk.* We have argued that a key dimension in considering an offender's future prospects must be a realistic appraisal of the risk of re-offending (see Chapter 5).

3 *No magic solutions.* We have argued in this chapter that report writers, in presenting community options to the court, should explicitly acknowledge that their suggestions cannot guarantee success, but are based upon constructive suggestions geared to achievable change.

In elaboration of this point, we would like to suggest a test for SIR practice developed during discussions on the RSDO course: this was 'doing the best for and with the defendant that can be done in the circumstances'. This implies social work empathy, and standing shoulder to shoulder with the defendant, yet it explicitly acknowledges the negative parts of the picture presented by the defendant's present situation and past history. It seeks to do the best for the defendant that can be done, not to present unachievable options.

4 *Enforcing supervisory disposals.* We have so far discussed 'credibility' simply through the medium of the SIR itself. We should add, however, that we consider an important additional element of credibility to lie in what happens subsequently to defendants placed on supervisory orders by the court. Discussion with various magistrates, and a judge, in the course of developing the ideas in this book highlighted a general concern with the issue of enforcement of supervisory orders, especially probation and supervision orders. It was felt that the court, in order to have the

confidence to make such orders, needed to be reassured that the defendant would adhere to the terms of the order, and that failure to do so would be taken seriously by the supervising officer, resulting if necessary in breach proceedings. The sentencers we consulted added that perhaps this was one reason why many benches preferred community service orders to probation orders: they felt they would be more seriously enforced.

Some important points have to be made here. On the one hand, we fully agree that enforcement should be taken seriously. On the other hand, we do not think it is in anyone's interest (the court, the client, the community or the probation service) to rush straight into court with breach proceedings whenever a client fails to meet any requirement of the order. Failure without good reason should never be condoned by the officer, but there are often sensible and low-key ways of dealing with it short of breach proceedings, and most courts well recognize this. When such methods have been tried unsuccessfully, formal warning letters and breach should follow, and this should enhance officers' general credibility with the courts.[12]

There is of course a very important difference between the four matters listed above, which we see as central to the 'credibility' dimension of our major question, and the traditional common understanding of the 'credibility' issue. The common understanding by courts locates 'credibility' simply in so-called 'realistic recommendations to the court', and this in turn is often a coded way of saying that custodial recommendations are not made as often as they should be; all too often this understanding has been taken up and adopted by report writers and their agencies. The basic problem with this view is that 'credibility' is seen by sentencers (and mirrored by report writers) as residing *only* in congruence between recommendation and sentence. This leads to an unhealthy preoccupation with 'second-guessing' by report writers about what might be in the court's mind, and a process of report writing designed not to alienate the court;[13] yet this process tends completely to ignore the very important point that the task of the sentencer embraces more dimensions than, and is wholly different from, the task of the report writer (see Chapter 2). 'Credibility' needs to be rethought in a different way, and this is what we have attempted in the preceding discussion.

This point can be developed by reference to the writings of others. Roberts and Roberts (1982) argue that:

to achieve a level of credibility appropriate to those claiming to offer professional advice to sentencers requires the presentation of recommendations in a way that takes account of how far they are congruent with the estimated sentence, *but should not require constant agreement between report writer and sentencer.* What credibility does require, where such an agreement does not exist, is *an appropriate investment of effort in acknowledging and accounting for the lack of congruence and for the alternatives proposed.* [emphasis added]

In other words, report writers should be aware of the likely considerations in the court's mind, but should not allow their thinking to be dominated by them. Emphasis should rather be placed on an 'appropriate investment of effort' in arguing carefully for the options proposed, from a fully social work point of view.

Helpful as Roberts and Roberts's point is, it still does not show adequate recognition of the differing roles in the sentencing process of report writing and sentencer. This point is, however, made very well by Brian Harris (1979), a former leading clerk to the justices and writer on magistrates' courts, who fully endorses the Streatfeild Committee's view that probation officers' opinions,

> however frank and comprehensive they may be, relate to only one of the possible considerations in the court's mind. (para. 346)

From this clear recognition of the differing tasks of report writers and sentencers, Harris (p.79) goes on to consider, in a passage showing remarkable understanding of the dilemmas of probation practice, what the effect is *on the client* of not understanding the clear difference of tasks. *Inter alia*, he asks:

> if the probation officer 'recommends' prison and the court adopts his recommendation might not the client feel – justifiably – that he has been sentenced by the probation officer?

It is for this reason, among others, that a new understanding of 'credibility' is required.

Notes

1   There have, of course, been parallel developments, of a rather different sort, for juvenile offenders under 17.
2   See the cases cited in Thomas (1987, section D 2.3 (a)).
3   For the details of this development, and a useful critique, see Harris (1979).
4   This circular speaks of the probation officer making a 'review of sentencing options', but adds that if she 'feels able to make a specific recommendation' she should do so.
5   It is, of course, the task of the clerk of the court to inform the bench (where appropriate) of the range of legally-available sentencing possibilities.
6   This has not always been achieved in earlier practice. For example, Harris and Webb

(1987, p.111) in a study of supervision orders made in 1978 on male and female juvenile offenders, found that 'recommendations for supervision orders were rarely amplified by reference to what would actually be done if an order were made; nor did the courts blanch from making orders without such justifications'.

7   The omitted words in the middle of this quotation are 'at the lowest cost and'. In our view, considerations of cost should not influence a report writer in the way suggested by the DHSS.

8   We would prefer this formulation to that of the DHSS, namely 'proposals to eliminate or curtail future offending' (para. 102); this formulation seems too similar to that of the Streatfeild Committee, and runs into similar difficulties. We should perhaps also add that in our formulation 'risk-related need' of course includes not only needs related to risk of future offending, but also needs related to risk of damage consequential on offending or likely offending (see Chapter 5), though in the context of proposing community options this second kind of need should receive only secondary attention.

9   It should be noted, to the credit of the Inner London Probation Service, that it subsequently built on the Stanley and Murphy (1984) research by commissioning the Demonstration Unit team (see Chapter 1) who were much less parsimonious in recommending supervisory disposals in high-tariff cases. Most of the probation orders made in the Demonstration Unit's work had normal completions or an early discharge for good progress (Harraway *et al.* 1985).

10 The research of Hine *et al.* (1978) suggests that when an SIR recommends custody, this strongly influences the court towards making a custodial disposal. Pointing out possible adverse effects of custody is, however, by no means the same as recommending custody.

11 This comment is necessarily somewhat speculative because of a lack of research evidence about how sentencers view SIRs (for a summary see Bottoms and McWilliams 1986, pp.267-9). As the following text makes clear, however, our comment is based partly on discussions with a judge and with magistrates in the course of preparing this book.

12 It will be apparent from this discussion that we are not much in favour of the 'instant breach' procedures in, for example, some day centres, CSO schemes, and heavy-end intermediate treatment projects. These seem to be something of an over-reaction to the previous practice of not taking enforcement seriously enough.

13 On this point, and some of its implications, see especially Davies (1974).

7 Beyond individual practice

The earlier chapters of this book have been concerned almost exclusively with individual SIR practice. We have tried to suggest a structure within which that practice can most closely follow and express professional social work knowledge, skills and values, while at the same time remaining consistent with the demands placed upon the report writer by legislation and official guidance.

But to leave it at that would be to imply that report writing takes place in some kind of a vacuum, and that the writer herself works without reference to, for example, the organizational context of her own agency, or the relationship between her agency and local courts. Thus, in this final chapter it is right to give attention, at least briefly, to the second two contexts within which SIR practice occurs, as highlighted by Tutt and Giller (1984), and as already referred to in Chapter 2. These are the contexts of, first, the report writer's own agency (organizational context). and, secondly, aspects of the criminal justice system beyond the report writer's own agency (systems context). Within the systems context, special attention must be paid to the relationship with the court.

This extension of perspective 'beyond individual practice' is in our view essential if individual practice itself is to be developed in the optimum way. In a nutshell, the purpose of this wider perspective is to see how probation services and social services departments can best sanction, support and reinforce SIR practice in the most helpful way.

The organizational context
Within the report writer's own agency, two key issues in particular need to be addressed. The first is the question of policy concerning the cases upon which SIRs should be written; the second concerns agency mechanisms for reviewing the content of SIRs before they are presented to the court.

Upon whom should reports be written?
A social work agency, such as a probation service or social service

department, is in the business of providing social work reports to courts. But the agency has resource constraints, and therefore needs to deploy its court-based services in the most effective and appropriate manner. How should this be achieved?

We would suggest, in the first place, that given the relevant statutory provisions (see Chapter 1), if a court specifically requests a *post-trial SIR*, this should be provided. A court clearly has the statutory power to make such a request, and, if it does so, it is the duty of the service or department to comply. That does not mean that courts should be encouraged to make indiscriminate requests of this sort; they should not. Rather, agencies should encourage courts to make such requests only in the following circumstances:

(a) where the offence and/or the defendant's record places him in a relatively high tariff position, and in particular where he is at serious risk of receiving a custodial sentence; and

(b) where for other reasons the court considers that a social work report may be appropriate and helpful (for example, where the offence appears to have occurred as a result of family conflict).

Turning now to *pre-trial reports,* that is reports prepared on the initiative of the probation service or social services department without a specific request from the court, we think that these have to be separately considered in relation to the three different kinds of court for whom they may be prepared: namely, the magistrates' court, the juvenile court and the Crown Court.

In the *magistrates' court* we can see no reason for any extensive provision of pre-trial reports. Magistrates can be encouraged to seek post-trial reports in the kind of cases set out above, and this should prove sufficient to provide an adequate SIR service for appropriate cases. The only routine exception to this that we would make would be in respect of current statutory clients of the agency whose current offence puts their order, their liberty or both at risk: in such cases, it seems clearly appropriate that the court should be entitled, at the first hearing, to see a report from the supervising agency.

There are two particular advantages to be gained from this kind of restrictive policy as regards pre-trial reports. First, it may encourage probation officers and social workers to think creatively about supervision possibilities for more difficult clients rather than those with few problems, by contrast with the Inner London research discussed in Chapter 6, where 'probation officers were directing their recommendations for supervision ... towards offenders with short or non-existent criminal records [and] those whose needs were perhaps more immediate and easier to meet' (Stanley and Murphy 1984, p. 34). Secondly, some research in the juvenile field suggests that the routine provision of SIRs for offenders in court for the first time may encourage courts to make supervisory disposals at an early point in the criminal career (rather than a fine or conditional discharge); and this may have the effect not only of deploying scarce social worker resources where they may not be really needed, but also possibly of hastening the imposition of higher-tariff sentences if the offender re-offends (Baldwin 1982; Tutt and Giller 1985).

Turning now to *juvenile courts,* traditionally pre-trial report preparation has been much more extensive in such courts than in magistrates' courts. Practice has, however, begun to change, particularly in the light of considerations such as those outlined in the previous paragraph. We would support such a change of practice, for we can see no overriding reason why policy should be different in magistrates' and juvenile courts. For the juvenile courts also, therefore, we would adopt a rule that no pre-trial reports should be prepared except in the case of current statutory clients whose current offence puts their order, their liberty or both at risk. This is in line with recent guidance from the DHSS.[1]

We would add one rider to the above. Busy courts understandably sometimes want to pass straight to the sentencing stage in cases where, for one reason or another, a probation officer's or social worker's report might well be helpful (as in the example given above concerning offences arising from family conflict). The court duty officer needs to be aware of this kind of situation, and should be willing where appropriate to make a suggestion for a report to the bench, or to ask for a short 'stand-down' period to talk to the defendant in order to satisfy herself whether or not a report would be helpful. It should go without saying that such interventions should be made selectively, and not in such a manner that they overturn the principles set out above. In effect, what we are suggesting is that the court duty officer's task is to try to ensure that the court is selecting the right cases for post-trial reports, in accordance with the principles that have been suggested.

That leaves us, finally, with the *Crown Court.* Since the expansion of SIR provision created by the Streatfeild Report (1961), pre-trial reports in the Crown Court have become the norm. Should they remain so?

Two considerations of special importance in the Crown Court are first, the higher cost of proceedings and therefore the need to reduce second hearings so far as possible (which we could see as an important, but not overriding consideration); and, secondly, the fact that those defendants who intend to plead guilty at the Crown Court have usually committed an offence of some gravity, and are therefore at some risk of receiving a custodial penalty. In the light of these considerations, we think that all defendants at Crown Court should have pre-trial reports prepared on them, with the following exceptions:

(a) those defendants who are pleading not guilty to the charge(s), or whose plea is uncertain, or whose plea of guilty is accompanied by a disputed fact central to the offence admitted (see Chapter 4):
(b) those defendants involved at the the more trivial end of 'multi-hander' offences, whose current offence(s) and previous history make it likely that they would have been dealt with summarily in the lower court without the need for a report, but who have gone to the Crown Court automatically because of the much more serious offences committed by their co-defendants.

In this connection, we can usefully make two comments on Home Office Circular 92/1986 (see Chapter 1 for an outline of the main points of this Circular). First, the arguments for not preparing SIRs for those intending to plead not guilty have been well rehearsed and expounded over the years, and they have recently been summarily put in the DHSS (1987) practice guidance booklet:

> There is a continuing debate about whether SIRs should be prepared before a finding of guilt has been established. Clearly, reports cannot be offence-focused if the [defendant] denies the offence. (para. 140)

Quite so. This argument seemed to be supported and endorsed in the original draft of HOC 92/1986, but this position was less clearly sustained in the final text (see Chapter 1). We find this regrettable, and would firmly endorse a policy of avoiding the preparation of pre-trial reports where the defendant is intending a not guilty plea.[2]

Secondly, we disagree strongly with the statement in the 1986 Circular that SIRs 'should not be prepared... in cases of serious and repeated offending where a custodial sentence is virtually inevitable' (para. 17).[3] To follow such an approach would be effectively to abandon the third core social work value of hope for the future. In addition it would, in our view rather arrogantly, be attempting to take on the sentencing role, which properly belongs to the court.[4]

Case example E

One case example should be sufficient to demonstrate the short-sightedness of this part of the Home Office Circular. This concerns Mr Craig, a 42-year-old man who appeared at the Crown Court on three charges of burglary and four of theft. The burglaries were all executed in an organized and well-planned way with a group of three others, all of whom had long criminal records. Mr Craig himself had appeared in court on 14 previous occasions, and had served six sentences of imprisonment, the longest of which was for four and a half years, though he had no previous convictions for offences of burglary. After an extensive and detailed account of his current offences and previous offending, the report went on to discuss Mr Craig's social situation, and especially his relationship with his cohabitee, a Mrs Poynton:

8   The difficulty in unravelling Mr Craig's currrent offending is matched by the complexity of his domestic situation. He is a married man with three children of the marriage, Melanie (11), Jimmy (4) and Lee (3). In July 1984 Mrs Craig left her husband and took all three children with her. A couple of months later I understand that she decided to leave Jimmy with him. In August 1984 Mr Craig and Mrs Poynton formed their relationship and Mrs Poynton, while retaining the tenancy of her Denton home, moved in with Mr Craig and Jimmy. With her came her three children, Louise (11), Naomi (9) and James (2). All three children are on the Non-Accidental Register in Denton because of an injury Mrs Poynton had inflicted on Louise some time before.

9   In November 1984 Mr Craig and Mrs Poynton had an argument, as a result of which she returned to Denton. It was at that time that Mr Craig began committing the offences for which he appears today. In March 1985 Mrs Craig returned to the matrimonial home bringing Melanie and Lee with her. The reconciliation did not last however, and she left again in June 1985. It would appear that she asked social services to deal with Jimmy, and he was returned to his father's care where he has remained ever since. In the same month Mrs Poynton returned to Bradlow [Mr Craig's home village] and resumed her relationship with Mr Craig. Thus at present the household comprises Mr Craig and Mrs Poynton, Jimmy and Mrs Poynton's three children.

10   Currently Mr and Mrs Craig are involved in a custody dispute which is due to be heard at the local domestic court next month. Clearly the probability of a custodial sentence for Mr Craig will affect the decision regarding Jimmy's care.

11   Mr Craig has been employed by the National Coal Board since 1978. His net take-home pay for regular shifts is approximately £90 per week after deductions have been made at source for his rent (£15 per week), a standing order for £10 per week, and repayment of a National Coal Board loan at £7.60 per week. In addition Mr Craig pays £20 per week hire purchase on various electrical items and £15 per week maintenance for his wife and younger son.

12 The village in which Mr Craig lives is a very close-knit mining community in which residents prefer to sort out their own problems rather than have recourse to statutory agencies. The social services involvement in Mr Craig's affairs concerning his and Mrs Poynton's children is seen by Mr Craig and some of his co-defendants as unnecessary and unwarranted interference. While there is clearly a spirit of mutual help in the village, in which Mr Craig and Mrs Poynton appear to play a full part, Mr Craig's younger reputation as a 'hard man' still lingers and local people are, therefore, somewhat wary of him and what he acknowledges used to be a very unpredictable temper. Because, unlike many of his co-defendants, he has not got a large family in the village, Mr Craig is something of a loner and depends heavily for company and emotional security on Mrs Poynton.

13 Mr Craig, Mrs Poynton and I spent some time discussing Mr Craig's extensive offending career, trying to answer my question to him of 'why do you offend?' Clearly financial reasons were a partial motive behind these current offences and doubtless several in the past. But his emotional upset of the past year was also a contributing factor. Mr Craig admitted how much he disliked living on his own, thus he was very disturbed when Mrs Poynton left him. Yet his behaviour over the past twenty-five years – of regularly committing offences and being sent to prison – has ensured that if he continues in that way he will ultimately always be left on his own. For he acknowledges that it is unreasonable to expect his wife or his cohabitee to stand by him and bring up his family alone, when he behaves criminally and thus gets removed from the domestic responsibilities he ought to be undertaking as a father and husband or cohabitee.

14 Mr Craig described himself as someone who had 'always been in trouble'; yet he denied my speculation that offending seemed to be addictive for him. There is though a sense in which the excitement of offending helps him feel young and connected with his youthful image of the daredevil hard man.

In terms of his offences and his previous record, Mr Craig could be considered likely to go to prison without any question; and if the 1986 Circular is right, the lengthy task of preparing the report should have been dispensed with, and the energy used on a more 'promising' case instead. The report went on to acknowledge the likelihood of such a sentence, but nevertheless to argue for a consideration of alternative possibilities, in the following manner:

Sentencing options:
15 Mr Craig fully expects to be sent to prison today. He states that prison will not deter him from further wrong-doing, merely put him in contact with other criminals while inside. There are other consequences of a prison sentence. First, he would lose his job if the sentence were of any length and

in the present climate, and given his age, he would be unlikely to be re-employed by the NCB on release.

16 Secondly, there is the question of Jimmy. The local social services department has said it will not permit Mrs Poynton to look after Jimmy on her own because of her assault on one of her children. The plan therefore is to put Jimmy into Mr Craig's sister-in-law's home (in Bradlow) on a normal fostering basis. This would enable Jimmy to keep close contact with Mrs Poynton and her children, continue to attend his school and go with Mrs Poynton to see his father as often as prison visits permitted. Social services have intimated that should Mr Craig get a long prison sentence they would seriously consider putting Jimmy into local authority care rather than the family fostering arrangement. This would clearly threaten Jimmy's stability. The other most likely consequence of a prison sentence is the threat it would place on Mr Craig's and Mrs Poynton's already quite volatile relationship.

17 Mr Craig's recognition of and resignation to the likelihood of a custodial sentence, and his seeming inability to identify *how* he could change, whilst at the same time saying that he has reached an age and a time in his life when he wants to change his ways, all bear the classic hallmarks of the 'old lag'. In terms of protecting society, the clearest short-term solution is to incarcerate Mr Craig, but such action in the past has proved no deterrent and would have several important, indeed destructive, consequences to his present social situation.

18 Any alternative course of action would present risks in terms of further wrongdoing but would have the advantage of involving Mr Craig in trying to change his attitudes and behaviour towards crime. Two possibilities present themselves for consideration. Statutory community supervision consisting of regular (weekly) meetings and in which any failure to keep to the requirements would lead to him being returned to court immediately, would offer Mr Craig a forum in which he would have to examine his behaviour in ways that might be distinctly uncomfortable for him. He said he would also value the opportunity of having an outside person to help him and Mrs Poynton with the normal problems attached to bringing up a diverse family and being in a newish and sometimes fragile adult relationship. He said he would also find it helpful for a probation officer to act as neutral intermediary between his household and the social services department.

19 The other option would be a community service order. While Mr Craig is skilled in a variety of ways and could put those skills to good community use, a community service order might stretch him more if he has to work with obviously disadvantaged *people* rather than simply with materials. Tasks of diverse kinds are available for a long order and Mr Craig has been deemed suitable for such work by the community service organizer.

The likelihood of imprisonment for Mr Craig was increased when it became known that his case was to be heard by one of the most severe judges on the relevant circuit, and one whose rapport with the local probation service left something to be desired. Yet, in the event, the judge commented on the helpfulness of the report, and then deferred sentence. When Mr Craig reappeared six months later, he was placed on probation for three years, the only requirement being that the probation officer had to provide three-monthly progress reports to the judge, who himself reserved the right to deal with any breaches of the order.

Reviewing the content of SIRs
In the juvenile justice field, many social services departments have established procedures for the monitoring of SIRs, usually by a senior officer or a court officer of the local authority, before the report is submitted to the court. These procedures are often familiarly referred to as 'gatekeeping' measures. The purpose of the procedures is to ensure that reports do not contain material which is considered inappropriate or irrelevant, and that they include the strongest possible arguments for non-custodial disposals in high-tariff cases. In some areas, a case conference may be held in order to ensure that all alternative programmes have been explored before the report is submitted. Additionally, if a recommendation in an SIR is not accepted by the court, and a custodial sentence is imposed, a 'post-mortem' may be held within the department to see what modifications to the form and content of SIRs might be appropriate in the future. (See generally Morris and Giller 1987, pp. 223-5.)

We believe that the introduction of monitoring procedures of this kind would have much to offer in the context of reports on adult offenders, as well as juveniles, though such a development would need to recognize and take into account the different organizational structure of the probation service as opposed to social services departments. But in advocating such an extension of 'gatekeeping', we are not blind to some of the problems which it may create. In the first place, SIRs are often prepared under considerable pressure of time (see Chapter 1), and therefore to introduce this additional procedural step requires careful organizational support for the report writer. Secondly, the use of senior officers as 'gatekeepers' creates, as the DHSS report admits, 'an area of potential conflict between report writer and manager' (DHSS 1987, para. 89). Thirdly, existing systems sometimes seem to focus their energy exclusively upon criticizing bad practice rather than commending good practice, which is not the best way to maximize basic-grade staff morale. Some of these latter difficulties could perhaps be overcome by report writers pairing with one another for the purpose of gatekeeping; or by forming a small gatekeeping panel for peer review; or by bringing all reports – or those within specified criteria – to team meetings for discussion, resolution or appraisal. The added value of some of these arrangements is that they may help a team to develop a more united sense of its professional purpose in SIR writing, and greater confidence in understanding key parts of that practice. Such corporate development should also help to create a culture in which both praise and criticism can occur.

If professional practice is to be enhanced by the kind of activity described above, we think it is crucial that it is backed up by an organizational statement from senior management in the agency. Such a statement would need to emphasize that monitoring is an essential part of SIR preparation and submission, and not simply an indulgence, or a 'luxury at a time of limited resources'.

We are aware that the suggestion of monitoring – whatever form it takes – inevitably raises the question of a potential threat to professional autonomy. This is not the place to enter into a general discussion about the merits or otherwise of this notion. Suffice it to say that it is a concept considered by probation officers in particular to have an almost sacrosanct value, and it undoubtedly brings to the probation task immense job satisfaction. But we would argue that the high morale which is a corollory of such satisfaction cannot be justified if it exists at the expense of the best possible service to clients, and that such a service can only be established by the kind of organizational accountability that is implied by the term 'monitoring'. For as Davies (1984) succinctly said: 'There is nothing inherently good about job autonomy if the work is not effective'.

The systems context
As we said at the beginning of this chapter, it is crucial to look not only at the internal organizational changes necessary to promote the best possible SIR practice, but to look also at those areas beyond the agency in which practice can be refined. In the juvenile context, an excellent illustration of this point concerns the relationship between SIRs and the school reports presented to juvenile courts (see Morris and Giller 1987, pp.225-7 for a discussion of this issue). Similarly, better links and consultation between the probation service and other local agencies such as psychiatric or educational services could clearly enhance consistency in practice, and help to overcome the

perennial problem of suggestions being made to the court without adequate prior consultation.

However, in considering the 'systems context' beyond the agency, our main concern is with what we would see as the central issue of the relationship between the report writing agency (be it probation or social services) and the court itself, the recipient of the report.

It is encouraging to note that in Home Office Circular 92/1986 a *professional* court presence is advocated, and, further, that 'area probation services' (and we interpret that phrase as meaning management headquarters in areas) are exhorted to enable probation officers, rather than simply 'probation staff', to occupy the role of court duty once again (para. 25). In saying this we intend no slight to the work of probation service assistants. But we do see it as a welcome attempt to reverse the trend of the probation service sliding from (in McWilliams's (1981) telling phrase) 'friend to acquaintance' in the court context. Unfortunately, the 1986 Circular is ambiguous in its meaning: it is not clear whether the availability of a 'probation officer' in court refers to the report writer herself, or to a court duty officer.

We think it is consistent with the values underpinning the entire SIR process that the report writer should, whenever possible, herself be present in court. We realize that by saying this, we run the risk of being accused of living in an unreal world. We can hear some hard-pressed probation officers and social workers asking whether we are aware of the many pressures and demands of their daily work; and we can see some cost-effectiveness-conscious managers raising their eyebrows at the apparent waste of resource time our suggestion implies.

Our answer to this is quite simple. Normative choices have to be made daily in many different spheres of human activity. Such choices demand clear value-commitments, and some of these commitments (including, in the present context, a commitment to the core social work values outlined in Chapter 3) may sometimes get in the way of the kind of pragmatism that is so often the hallmark of organizational decision-making. This is an occasion when pragmatism needs to be checked to further the best possible practice, and it is encouraging that recent documents seem to be beginning to recognize this.[5] Thus, in our view, ensuring that report writers attend court with defendants should again become a priority, and should become the agency's (and not the individual practitioner's) responsibility to organize. One way in which agencies can promote this is by holding discussions with courts, at appropriate levels of seniority, about the listing of cases at court. There is ample evidence that courts welcome the presence of the report writer at the time of sentence; but the organization of courts tends not to take report writers' time into account, so that much valuable professional time may be wasted.

The core social work values not only require the report writer's presence in court whenever possible, they also require that the relationship with the defendant *vis-à-vis* the court appearance takes certain forms. Thus, as argued in Chapter 4, there needs to be a thorough explanation of the SIR process if 'respect for the defendant' is to be observed. Since the same core value requires that the defendant has an adequate opportunity to be aware of the content of the report, and to comment upon it, time needs to be set aside before the day of the court appearance to share it with him. In addition, if the report is to be read silently by the bench in open court or by retiring (as is common practice in magistrates' courts), it is courteous to ensure that the defendant also has a copy to re-read at the same time.

The court duty officer's role should incorporate all the above, but it should also include careful liaison with the report writer (this being the report writer's responsibility, not the duty officer's) together with contact with the defendant both before and after the hearing.

If the report writer is to be truly a 'friend of the court', it is important that the court should be aware of her presence, and should be encouraged to invite further comment or ask clarificatory questions about the report. Similarly, if the report writer has any supplementary points to make, she should not feel inhibited in rising to comment. It is not sufficient, in our view, for the author to hand in her report, sit silently in court, and assume that the task of court attendance has been properly accomplished. Another, more direct way of ensuring that the author's presence is positive, in the magistrate's court, is for the report writer to hand in her report from the witness box as a matter of course. The principle of an active and engaged presence remains a valuable one to be striven for in all courts if the concept of 'friend of the court' is to be taken seriously. We would add that by acting in this way the concept is extended to include being a 'friend *at* court' to the defendant, by ensuring that concern for the defendant and his interests is not allowed to go by default in silence.

If the kind of practice suggested above – and indeed throughout this book – is to be developed, several things need to happen. Probation services and social services departments need to construct and then stand by clear policy statements about the primacy of the

SIR task and about desirable kinds of SIR practice. This is particularly important in supporting and reinforcing the position of the individual officer *vis-à-vis* the courts.

Secondly, the organizations, as well as individuals or teams, have a responsibility to bring to local courts' attention information both about the range of community disposals available, and relevant statistical information about the way in which they are being used (for example, about types of offender the court is putting on probation). Organizations can also take a more proactive role in promoting appropriate workshops, seminars, etc. for magistrates and judges.

As well as the above, Chief Probation Officers and Directors of Social Services can encourage links at clerk and judge level, in addition to creating better links between benches from different Petty Sessional Divisions within their geographical areas. In terms of the probation service, it would also be useful for higher managers to attend probation liaison meetings on a more regular basis than is often thought necessary at present.

Participants in local discussions of the sort suggested above often find themselves debating the time-honoured question, raised in Chapter 1, of whether the report writer is primarily an officer of the court or a social worker with offenders. In the light of the argument of this book, we think that this issue can be resolved. We believe that a clear focus upon risk, and risk-related need, makes it perfectly possible to be both, so long as courts are willing to accept that, as a social worker, the report writer has knowledge, skills and values which have a clear and relevant place in the court's concerns; and, by the same token, so long as organizations accept that, as officers of the court, their staff have certain obligations and duties, for example, as regards the enforcement of orders (see Chapter 6). Such bilateral acceptance must depend upon a clear mutual understanding that the two parties have different, though complementary, roles and functions in the criminal justice system. The report writer's role and function derives from her social work perspective (see Chapter 3); the court's role and function is as the representative of the whole community. From a common understanding such as this, the two parties should be able to recognize that they share interdependent interests in an important public activity, in which there can be close co-operation so long as clear role differentiation is acknowledged.

Conclusion

We hope that this chapter goes some way towards setting report writing in a broader organizational context, and so freeing report writers from feelings of professional isolation. Ensuring the best possible professional practice is a joint responsibility of both the individual practitioner and her organization. Practice is sure to founder, and practitioners are sure to become disenchanted or burnt out without both members of the partnership acting responsibly and in concert.

Endnote

A book can be finished in many ways. We were tempted to try to conclude on an intellectually neat note, and that might have been satisfying at one level. But to have done this would somehow have been to deny the living and dynamic nature of social inquiry work, and to deny also the 'messiness of practice' to which we referred in an earlier chapter. We have not presented the ideas in this book as some kind of immutable blueprint for SIR writing, or as the only possible kind of practice. But we have, throughout, tried to remain practice-oriented. We dare to hope that our suggestions may help to enhance professional confidence and competence, and to foster a greater clarity about the task of preparing well-argued SIRs which are credible social work documents.

Notes

1   See DHSS (1987, paras 2, 96, 140-42). The clearest policy statement is in para. 2 ('in the majority of cases ... pre-trial reports do not best serve the interests of children'), but this statement is not supported by detailed argument.

2   A possible minor exception to this is where the defendant is charged with one or more major offences, to which he intends to plead guilty, together with a minor offence to which he intends to plead not guilty. In such circumstances, a report could be prepared covering the major offence(s) only.

3   See also the joint statement by the Association of Chief Officers of Probation (ACOP), the Central Council of Probation Committees and the National Association of Probation Officers, which on this point stated: 'we do not accept ... that reports are wasted in cases where custody is "inevitable": in our experience this is far from predictable, and in any case reports may provide information which enables sentencers to shorten sentences, an important general goal in the criminal justice system' (ACOP *et al.* 1987, p.6).

4   It should be noted, of course, that not producing a report at all is a different policy option from preparing a report without any suggested community options (on which point see Chapter 6, p.100).

5   The DHSS booklet on *Reports to Courts* advises that 'wherever possible the author of a report should attend the hearing. This almost invariably happens in care but not in criminal proceedings' (DHSS 1987, para. 42). The document sponsored by three probation-based associations (see note 3 above) states that 'there is common agreement that it would be helpful for probation officers, where possible, to attend court with their reports, at least in difficult cases. This would clearly require an extra commitment of time, even if court practices were changed' (ACOP *et al.* 1987, p.6).

Appendix

At the end of Chapter 5, we offered a rewritten version of an SIR for Mr Green, the actual report for whom (written in 1982) is printed in Chapter 1. In this Appendix, we present rewritten versions of the other two 1982 reports reproduced in Chapter 1, namely the reports on Mr Bishop and Mr Davenport. In presenting these, we should point out that we are not assuming that reports should have been asked for by the court in either case: it is arguable that, by the criteria listed in Chapter 7, the court would not necessarily request a report for either Mr Bishop or Mr Davenport. On the assumption that a report was requested, however, reports of the following kind are suggested.

Name: Andrew Bishop (aged 49)
Offence: Assist in handling stolen goods
Information relevant to offending and previous offences:
   1 Mr Bishop told me that the offence occurred as a result of his going to a public house which used to be his 'local' before he and his family moved home last year. He continues to go there because it is where the allotment society meets of which he is a long-standing and highly-respected member, holding the position of show-organizer. On the evening in question he said he was approached by an acquaintance of one of the club members. He was asked if he would 'look after' several electrical items for a couple of weeks and was told, presumably as an inducement to do so: 'there would be a few pounds in it for you'. I asked Mr Bishop why he thought he had been picked out to do this. He said that a few weeks earlier in the same pub, he had mentioned how hard up he was. Three days after the goods had been brought to his house the police came and interviewed him. All the goods were then recovered.
   2 At the time the offences were committed (10 months ago) the Bishop family was enduring financial hardship. Mr Bishop's benefit had just been lost through an administrative oversight at the local DHSS office; and his wife and two older children (20 and 16 years), all of whom work at the local bakery, had been put on short time for a two-month period. Having told me this Mr Bishop was anxious during our interviews that I should not think he was trying to excuse his action. He expressed remorse for his behaviour in terms of having let himself and his family down very badly.

3   His only previous offence was committed five years ago against his then employer, a security firm. Although he appears to have played a minor part in that criminal venture (his co-defendants received two and three' imprisonment) his abuse of trust was deemed serious enough to warrant a six-month sentence of immediate imprisonment.

Social information relevant to offending:

4   Since his release from prison Mr Bishop has not been able to find regular employment and is thus dependent on state benefit for his income. He receives £62 per week supplementary benefit. In addition his wife collects £4.50 per week child benefit for Susan (13 years old). His two older children John (20) and Paul (16) both contribute £12 per week from their earnings, and Mrs Bishop herself earns £27 per week in her part-time job. Mr Bishop pays a subsidized rent of £9.50 per week, and the family also have HP arrangements amounting to approximately £13 per week.

5   Prior to his period of imprisonment Mr Bishop had been in employment in several capacities. Most notable was his job with the NCB, which ended in 1974 because of an industrial accident to his back. Though this did not prevent Mr Bishop taking up a security job, he lost this when he was sent to prison and it has since proved impossible to get further full-time employment. He now divides his time between helping in the house, gardening and undertaking his role in the allotment society. Both Mr Bishop and his wife describe their marriage as a happy partnership.

6   Mr Bishop is angry that he has compromised his family's standing in the locality by this further criminal act. He recognizes that just as his family had stood by and supported him during this crisis, the community has acted similarly towards them. But he is also very well aware that further transgressions could stretch his wife's tolerance beyond its limit, and this knowledge may well be the most effective deterrent against further wrong-doing.

7   Financial hardship has been a recent preoccupation for the family, and is the underlying reason for the commission of this and his one previous offence. It is a demonstration of the strength of his avowal not to offend further that Mr Bishop, on his own initiative, has been to the Citizen's Advice Bureau to find out about a basic money management course. He has now made contact with the group in his area that deals with this kind of problem, and has already enrolled in it. While this cannot guarantee that Mr Bishop will not offend again, it is a clear indication that Mr Bishop is attempting to make every effort to minimize the likelihood of re-offending.

Options:

8   The sizeable gap between this offence and his previous crime does not suggest that Mr Bishop is embarking on a criminal career. Rather, it appears to be an isolated act of thoughtlessness and stupidity prompted not by acquisitiveness but by financial hardship. In such circumstances the court may be looking at the minimum disposals as sufficient penalties. Two come to mind. A fine taking account of his existing commitments and

financial position is one option. By his recent actions he has demonstrated that he is able to seek appropriate help in order to manage his financial affairs.

9   The other option is a conditional discharge. This would have the merit of keeping Mr Bishop's mind focused on the fact that he offended for the next one or two years; but it would also acknowledge that he is making efforts to overcome his problem in a courageous and relevant manner. From my contact with Mr Bishop and his family I do not consider that a probation order would be necessary, since the relevant areas of need can be handled adequately by Mr Bishop on a voluntary basis.

Name: Barry Davenport (aged 17)
Offences:
1   Drive while disqualified
2   No insurance
3   No test certificate
Information relevant to offending and previous offences:
1   Barry Davenport appears today on three road traffic act charges. He explained to me that the offences were all connected with the car that he owned. It was normally parked outside his house, and he is adamant that he had never driven it before this offence: he had only used it to refine his already considerable mechanical skills. On this occasion some local youths had 'borrowed' the car and stripped it of some of its parts. Mr Davenport wanted to return it to its normal parking place, so he simply – and clearly without thinking about the consequences – got in and drove it the six miles to his home.

2   Mr Davenport has appeared before the court on two previous occasions. The first time was for a shoplifting offence from a car parts shop, for which he received a fine. This followed hard on the heels of a similar act some two months before, for which he had been cautioned. Then in July 1981 he was convicted of driving a car with excess alcohol, driving under age, and allied offences such as no insurance. He received a two-year ban and a total fine of £90, of which he has so far repaid £36 to the court.
Social situation relevant to offending:
3   For the past year Mr Davenport has lived with his mother and half-brother Andrew Smith. His other half-brother Arthur is currently serving a prison sentence and Andrew himself has only just returned home from custody.

4   The defendant was born two years after his mother had separated from Mr Smith, and during her longstanding, frequently interrupted and highly-volatile cohabitation with Barry's father, Mr Davenport senior. At the age of one, Barry Davenport was received, with his half-brothers, into local authority care. Contact was quickly lost between the three parents (Mrs Smith as she then was, Mr Smith and Mr Davenport senior) and the three boys.

5 The boys remained together in the local authority establishment for six years, after which they were placed, again all together, with foster parents. For the five years that followed that placement neither their mother nor their fathers had any contact with them. The period of foster care ended abruptly when the foster father was convicted of sexual assault against Andrew. At that point the three boys were separated, Barry Davenport returning to a local authority home where he remained until May 1979.

6 In 1978 Barry Davenport's parents married. It appears to have been his hope that, when he was eventually allowed home, he and his parents would be able to live as a 'proper family'. This was not to be, since shortly after the marriage Mr Davenport senior left his wife in order to start another relationship.

7 Barry Davenport was finally allowed to return home in 1979. His disappointment at his parents' separation, the difficulty he had in freeing himself of the inevitable problems of thirteen years of living in institutions, and his offending, all combined to make domestic reintegration very hard for him and his mother. Because of this he left home and went to live with a family friend, returning home about 11 months ago.

8 The above description clearly suggests a very turbulent and unsettled life in which the only periods of calm have been those offered by local authority institutions. Barry Davenport is also, and hardly surprisingly, much younger in attitude and behaviour than his age might suggest. Apart from a short period on the work experience programme he has remained unemployed since leaving school. He is somebody for whom it has been vitally important to have an idealized picture of family life to hold on to. He has found that the reality does not match the picture, hence his difficulties, especially with his mother.

9 There are many factors in Mr Davenport's life which make appropriate social behaviour even harder to attain than is usually the case with people of his age. His unsettled and quite damaging early life experience; the anger he clearly feels towards his mother for her perceived abandonment of him during those years; and her expressed feelings of guilt regarding that time, all mean they have difficult obstacles to overcome if they are to achieve some measure of family harmony. In such a context what is surprising is not that Mr Davenport has offended, but that he has offended so relatively infrequently.

Community options:

10 It may be that the court will consider that a financial or nominal sentence will be sufficient to mark the gravity of the present offences. In that event, and bearing in mind that the care order in this case expires shortly, it can be expected (on the basis of discussions held during the preparation of this report) that Barry Davenport and his mother will seek voluntary social work help with their difficulties of relationship. Both have said that they would be keen to be involved in this way.

11 Should the court take a more serious view of the offences, my

proposal to the court would be to consider a probation order of 12 months duration. If such an order were made, part of the work done would be supportive, in the classic role of 'advising, assisting and befriending'. Additionally, it would be important to work with Mr Davenport and his mother together so as to give them the opportunity to explore and express in a safe way some of their hostile feelings towards each other. Another, and more pragmatic focus for the order would be to involve Mr Davenport on a voluntary basis in the local 'banger group' (information leaflet attached). This would enable Mr Davenport to pursue his passion for cars in a safe and acceptable environment, and would provide him with the opportunity of helping some of the younger and less proficient members of the group. He has expressed his willingness to attend this group.

Bibliography

Abrams, P. (1978), 'Community Care: Some Research Problems and Priorities' in J. Barnes and N. Connelly (eds), *Social Care Research*, London: Bedford Square Press.

Association of Chief Officers of Probation, Central Council of Probation Committees, and National Association of Probation Officers (1987), *Probation – The Next Five Years*, London.

Baldwin, J. (1982), 'Scaling the Tariff Barrier', *Social Work Today*, Vol. 13, No. 34 (11 May), p.1.

Bartholomew, A.A. and Lord, D.E. (1975), 'The Pre-Sentence Report: Another Look', *Howard Journal of Penology and Crime Prevention*, Vol. 14, pp. 23-30.

Bottoms, A.E. (1980), 'An Introduction to the Coming Crisis' in A.E. Bottoms and R.H. Preston (eds), *The Coming Penal Crisis*, Edinburgh: Scottish Academic Press.

Bottoms, A.E. (1981), 'The Suspended Sentence in England 1967-1978', *British Journal of Criminology*, Vol. 21, pp. 1-26.

Bottoms, A.E. (1987), 'Limiting Prison Use: Experience in England and Wales', *Howard Journal of Criminal Justice*, Vol. 26, pp. 177-202.

Bottoms, A.E. and McClintock, F.H. (1973), *Criminals Coming of Age*, London: Heinemann Educational Books.

Bottoms, A.E. and McWilliams, W. (1979), 'A Non-Treatment Paradigm for Probation Practice', *British Journal of Social Work*, Vol. 9, pp. 159-202.

Bottoms, A.E. and McWilliams, W. (1986), 'Social Inquiry Reports Twenty-Five Years after the Streatfeild Report' in P. Bean and D. Whynes (eds), *Barbara Wootton, Social Science and Public Policy: Essays in Her Honour*, London: Tavistock Publications.

Brearley, C.P. (1982), *Risk and Social Work*, London: Routledge & Kegan Paul.

Brody, S.R. (1976), *The Effectiveness of Sentencing*, Home Office Research Study No. 35, London: HMSO.

Bryant, M., Coker, J., Estlea, B., Himmel, S. and Knapp, T. (1978), 'Sentenced to Social Work', *Probation Journal*, Vol. 25, pp. 110-14.

Burney, E. (1985a), 'All Things to All Men: Justifying Custody under the 1982 Act', *Criminal Law Review*, pp. 284-93.

Burney, E. (1985b), *Sentencing Young People*, Aldershot: Gower.

Celnick, A. (1984), 'Heeley Project Evaluation Report', unpublished report of the South Yorkshire Probation Service.

Central Council of Probation and After-Care Committees (1981), *Social Inquiry Reports*, London.

Clarke, D.H. (1978), 'Marxism, Justice and the Justice Model', *Contemporary Crises*, Vol. 2, pp. 27-62.

Cohen, S. (1985), *Visions of Social Control*, Cambridge: Polity Press.

Critcher, C. (1976), 'Structures, Cultures and Biographies' in S. Hall and T. Jefferson (eds), *Resistance Through Rituals*, London: Hutchinson.

Curnock, K. and Hardiker, P. (1979), *Towards Practice Theory*, London: Routledge & Kegan Paul.

Curran, J.H. and Chambers, G.A. (1982), *Social Inquiry Reports in Scotland*, Edinburgh: HMSO.

Davies, M. (1974), 'Social Inquiry for the Courts', *British Journal of Criminology*, Vol. 14, pp. 18-33.

Davies, M. (1981), *The Essential Social Worker* (1st ed.), London: Heinemann Educational Books.

Davies, M. (1984), 'Community-Based Alternatives to Custody: The Right Place for the Probation Service', *Prison Service Journal*, No. 53 (New Series), pp.2-5.

Davies, M. (1985), *The Essential Social Worker* (2nd ed.), Aldershot: Gower.

Department of Health and Social Security (1987), *Reports to Courts: Practice Guidance for Social Workers*, London: HMSO.

Donzelot, J. (1980), *The Policing of Families*, London: Hutchinson.

Duff, R.A. (1986), *Trials and Punishments*, Cambridge: Cambridge University Press.

Dworkin, R. (1977), *Taking Rights Seriously*, London: Duckworth.

Eaton, M. (1985), 'Documenting the Defendant: Placing Women in Social Inquiry Reports' in J. Brophy and C. Smart (eds), *Women in Law*, London: Routledge & Kegan Paul.

Eaton, M. (1986), *Justice for Women?*, Milton Keynes: Open University Press.

Emmins, C.J. (1985), *A Practical Approach to Sentencing*, London: Financial Training Publications.

Farrington, D.P. and Morris, A.M. (1983), 'Sex, Sentencing and Reconviction', *British Journal of Criminology*, Vol. 23, pp. 229-48.

Ford, P. (1972), *Advising Sentencers,* Oxford University Penal Research Unit Occasional Paper No. 5, Oxford: Basil Blackwell.

Foucault, M. (1977), *Discipline and Punishment,* London. Allen Lane.

Foucault, M. (1981), *The History of Sexuality,* Vol. 1, Harmondsworth: Penguin.

Garland, D. (1985), *Punishment and Welfare,* Aldershot: Gower.

Gewirth, A. (1978), *Reason and Morality,* Chicago: University of Chicago Press.

Haines, J. (1975), *Skills and Methods in Social Work,* London: Constable.

Harding, J. (1982), *Victims and Offenders,* NCVO Occasional Paper No. 2, London: Bedford Square Press.

Harding, J. (ed.) (1987), *Probation and the Community,* London: Tavistock Publications.

Harraway, P.C., Brown, A.J., Hignett, C.F., Wilson, I.O., Abbott, J.S., Mortimer, S.A. and Keegan, A.C. (1985), *The Demonstration Unit 1981-1985,* London: Inner London Probation Service.

Harris, B. (1979), 'Recommendations in Social Inquiry Reports', *Criminal Law Review,* pp. 73-81.

Harris, R. and Webb, D. (1987), *Welfare, Power and Juvenile Justice,* London: Tavistock Publications.

Heal, K. and Laycock, G. (eds) (1986), *Situational Crime Prevention: From Theory into Practice,* London: HMSO.

Hine, J., McWilliams, W. and Pease, K. (1978), 'Recommendations, Social Information and Sentencing', *Howard Journal of Penology and Crime Prevention,* Vol. 17, pp. 91-100.

Home Office (1983a), *Probation and After-Care: Implications of the Criminal Justice Act 1982,* Home Office Circular 4/1983, London: Home Office.

Home Office (1983b), *Social Inquiry Reports: General Guidance on Contents,* Home Office Circular 17/1983, London: Home Office.

Home Office (1983c), *Social Inquiry Reports: Recommendations Relevant to Sentencing,* Home Office Circular 18/1983, London: Home Office.

Home Office (1986), *Social Inquiry Reports:* Home Office Circular 92/1986, London: Home Office.

Home Office and Lord Chancellor's Office (1961), *Report of the Inter-departmental Committee on the Business of the Criminal Courts* (The Streatfeild Report), Cmnd. 1289, London: HMSO.

Horsley, G. (1984), *The Language of Social Inquiry Reports,* University of East Anglia Social Work Monograph No. 27, Norwich:

University of East Anglia.

Hudson, B. (1987), *Justice Through Punishment,* London: Macmillan.

Hugman, B. (1977), *Act Natural,* London: Bedford Square Press.

Jarvis, F.V. (1980), *Probation Officers' Manual* (3rd ed.), London: Butterworths.

McWilliams, W. (1981), 'The Probation Officer at Court: From Friend to Acquaintance', *Howard Journal of Penology and Crime Prevention,* Vol. 20, pp. 97-116.

McWilliams, W. (1986), *The English Social Inquiry Report: Development and Practice,* unpublished PhD thesis, University of Sheffield.

Matza, D. (1969), *Becoming Deviant,* Englewood Cliffs, N.J: Prentice-Hall.

Morris, A. and Giller, H. (1987), *Understanding Juvenile Justice,* London: Croom Helm.

National Association of Probation Officers (1981), *Social Inquiry Reports: A Policy Paper from N.A.P.O.,* London: NAPO.

Nuttall, C.P. (1977), *Parole in England and Wales,* Home Office Research Study No. 38, London: HMSO.

Paley, J. and Leeves, R. (1982), 'Some Questions about the Reverse Tariff', *British Journal of Social Work,* Vol. 12, pp. 363-80.

Parker, H., Jarvis, G. and Sumner, M. (1987), 'Under New Orders: The Redefinition of Social Work with Young Offenders', *British Journal of Social Work,* Vol. 17, pp. 21-43.

Paton, H.J. (1948), *The Moral Law: Kant's Groundwork of the Metaphysic of Morals,* London: Hutchinson.

Pease, K. (1985), 'Community Service Orders' in M. Tonry and N. Morris (eds), *Crime and Justice: An Annual Review of Research,* Vol. 6, Chicago: University of Chicago Press.

Perry, F.G. (1974), *Information for the Court,* Institute of Criminology Occasional Paper No. 1, Cambridge: Institute of Criminology.

Philpotts, G.J.O. and Lancucki, L.B. (1979), *Previous Convictions, Sentence and Reconvictions,* Home Office Research Study No. 53, London: HMSO.

Plummer, K. (1979), 'Misunderstanding Labelling Perspectives' in D. Downes and P. Rock (eds), *Deviant Interpretations,* Oxford: Martin Robertson.

Raynor, P. (1980), 'Is There Any Sense in Social Inquiry Reports?', *Probation Journal,* Vol. 27, pp. 78-84.

Raynor, P. (1981), 'Diagnosis and Description: Who Owns the

Problem?', *Probation Journal*, Vol. 28, pp. 39-43.

Raynor, P. (1985), *Social Work, Justice and Control*, Oxford: Basil Blackwell.

Reynolds, F. (1985), 'Magistrates' Justifications for Making Custodial Orders on Juvenile Offenders', *Criminal Law Review*, pp. 294-8.

Richardson, N. (1987), *Justice by Geography?*, Manchester: Social Information Systems.

Roberts, J. and Roberts, C. (1982), 'Social Inquiry Reports and Sentencing', *Howard Journal of Penology and Crime Prevention*, Vol. 21, pp. 76-93.

Smith, G. (1980), *Social Need: Policy, Practice and Research*, London: Routledge & Kegan Paul.

Soothill, K.L. and Pope, P.J. (1973), 'Arson: A Twenty-Year Cohort Study', *Medicine, Science and The Law*, Vol. 13, pp. 127-38.

Speller, A. (1986), *Breaking Out*, London: Hodder & Stoughton.

Stanley, S.J. and Murphy, B. (1984), *Inner London Probation Service: Survey of Social Enquiry Reports*, London: Inner London Probation Service.

Streatfeild Report (1961). See Home Office and Lord Chancellor's Office (1961).

Thomas, D.A. (ed.) (1987), *Current Sentencing Practice* (looseleaf encyclopedia, incorporating twelfth release), London: Sweet & Maxwell.

Tutt, N. and Giller, H. (1984), *Social Inquiry Reports*, Lancaster: Social Information Systems (tape-recording).

Tutt, N. and Giller, H. (1985), 'Doing Justice to Great Expectations', *Community Care*, 17 January, pp. 20-23.

Von Hirsch, A. (1986), *Past or Future Crimes*, Manchester: Manchester University Press.

Walker, H. and Beaumont, B. (1981), *Probation Work*, Oxford: Basil Blackwell.

Walker, N. (1980), *Punishment, Danger and Stigma*, Oxford: Basil Blackwell.

Walker, N. (1985), *Sentencing: Theory, Law and Practice*, London: Butterworths.

Whan, M. (1986), 'On the Nature of Practice', *British Journal of Social Work*, Vol. 16, pp. 243-50.

Whitehead, P. and Macmillan, J. (1985), 'Checks or Blank Cheque?', *Probation Journal*, Vol. 32, pp. 87-9.

Willis, A. (1986), 'Alternatives to Imprisonment: An Elusive Paradise?' in J. Pointing (ed.), *Alternatives to Custody*, Oxford: Basil Blackwell.

Wootton, B. (1981), *Crime and the Criminal Law* (2nd ed.), London: Stevens.

Subject index

Author index

135